Pressing On When You'd Rather Turn Back

Studies in Philippians

GENE A. GETZ

Regal Books

A Division of GL Publications
Ventura, California, U.S.A.

Published by Regal Books
A Division of GL Publications
Ventura, California 93006
Printed in U.S.A.

Formerly published under the title: *The Measure of a Christian—Studies in
Philippians.*

Library of Congress Cataloging in Publication Data

Getz, Gene A.
    The measure of a Christian.

    1. The Bible, N.T. Philippians—Text-books.
2. Christian life—1960-   I. Title
BS2705.2.G47   1983   227'.606   83-3002
ISBN 0-8307-0883-9

2 3 4 5 6 7 8 9 10 / 91 90 89 88

Rights for publishing this book in other languages are contracted by Gospel
Literature International (GLINT) foundation. GLINT also provides technical
help for the adaptation, translation, and publishing of Bible study resources
and books in scores of languages worldwide. For further information, contact
GLINT, Post Office Box 488, Rosemead, California, 91770, U.S.A., or the
publisher.

Contents

Preface

Christianity works! It's real! Jesus Christ *is* "the same yesterday, today and forever."

Right now you may be doubting this. You're frustrated. You need some reassurance. Maybe you feel persecuted and misunderstood — even laughed at and scorned. Or maybe you've been let down by someone — perhaps a fellow Christian. You're depressed and disillusioned.

How about your financial situation? Maybe you don't have enough "bread" on the table — and maybe you do!

Whatever the situation, you probably feel a little sorry for yourself. Welcome to the club: most Christians feel that way every once in a while.

But whatever your state, this book — and the Letter it explains — is written for you. Whatever your problem, there is a practical lesson in Paul's letter to the Philippian Christians that will apply to *your* life.

"But I don't have any problems!" you exclaim. That's okay. Let's study together anyway. But may I warn you! You may be aware of some problems afterward.

That need not scare you. Christians shouldn't be afraid of problems. Face reality. This book is designed to make you aware of personal problems. But more important, it's designed to help you to be a *growing* and *maturing* Christian in the midst of a very unpredictable world.

Paul lived in this kind of world: he was in prison. The Philippians, too, lived in this kind of world: they were persecuted by those who despised their Christian convictions. But Paul learned the secret of being "content whatever the circumstances" (Phil. 4:11). And he shared those secrets with the Philippian Christians. Let's discover what they were. They'll work for us, too!

GENE A. GETZ
Dallas, Texas

WHY THIS STUDY?

Most letters in the New Testament describe first-century churches—churches that were in the process of "developing the mind of Christ." Some were further along than others in this process of renewal.

The church of Philippi represents one of the most mature churches. Though they were far from perfect—every church is—the relationships were deep. They were experiencing unusual unity, and they were working hard at being a dynamic witness in the world.

Studying the book of Philippians is a must for every church desiring to experience biblical renewal. Paul's words are just as relevant today as they were the day he wrote them. Furthermore, there are dynamic lessons for every social unit in the church—the family, marital partners, as well as individual Christians.

RENEWAL—A BIBLICAL PERSPECTIVE

Renewal is the essence of dynamic Christianity and the basis on which Christians, both in a corporate or "body" sense and as individual believers, can determine the will of God. Paul made this clear when he wrote to the Roman Christians—"be transformed by the *renewing of your mind.*" Then he continued "you will be able to test and approve what God's will is" (Rom. 12:2). Here Paul is talking about renewal in a corporate sense. In other words, Paul is asking these Christians as a *body* of believers, to develop the mind of Christ through corporate renewal.

Personal renewal will not happen as God intended it unless it happens in the context of corporate renewal. On the other hand, corporate renewal will not happen as God intended without personal renewal. Both are necessary.

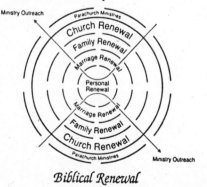

Biblical Renewal

The larger circle represents "church renewal." This is the most comprehensive concept in the New Testament. However, every local church is made up of smaller self-contained, but interrelated units. The *family* in Scripture emerges as the "church in miniature." In turn, the family is made up of an even smaller social unit—*marriage*. The third inner circle represents *personal* renewal, which is inseparably linked to all of the other basic units. Marriage is made up of two separate individuals who become one. The family is made up of parents and children who are also to reflect the mind of Christ. And the church is made up of not only individual Christians, but couples and families.

Though all of these social units are interrelated, biblical renewal can begin within any specific social unit. But wherever it begins—in the church, families, marriages or individuals—the process immediately touches all the other social units. And one thing is certain! All that God says is consistent and harmonious. He does not have one set of principles for the church and another set for the family, another for husbands and wives and another for individual Christians. For example, the principles God outlines for local church elders, fathers and husbands regarding their role as leaders are interrelated and consistent. If they are not, we can be sure that we have not interpreted God's plan accurately.

How to Make This Book Work for You

You can use this book in various ways.

Personal Study

First, you can read it by yourself — a chapter at a time. And you can read it straight through in one sitting if you like. But if you do only that, you'll miss the most important thing — the life response and follow-through.

Every chapter leads to a decision on your part — a twentieth-century application to your own life. But *you* must do the applying to your particular situation.

So you will want to study with book, Bible, notebook, and pencil in hand. And you will want to be prepared to think and meditate. That's why if you read it through in one or two sittings, you will need to consider this an overview. Then go back and read carefully one chapter at a time and work through each life response, probably not more than one a week. If you go further, you'll have more "to do" than you can personally handle.

Group Study

Personal study is great, and it may be your preference. But the real excitement will come in a group, as members of the body of Christ — in a Sunday school class, in midweek Bible study, a morning coffee hour. Read and discuss the material together. Work out the life responses. Share your personal goals and objectives and work through the group projects.

Family Bible Study

Once a week, with your children who are junior-high age (12 or above), study this book together. Set aside one evening and make it "family night."

A suggestion: Every member of the family should do his "homework" by reading each chapter and working out the life responses in private devotions. Then come together once a week to share your responses and to follow through on each suggested "family project."

Enjoy this book! Bible study *can* be exciting — especially when it changes your life.

The Format

Each chapter in this book is organized in several parts.

1. Something to Think About

How does *your* life — as you live in the twentieth century — relate to Lydia, the Philippian jailer, or other Christians who lived in Philippi in A.D. 62? To help bridge your thinking from the twentieth to the first century, each chapter begins with "Something to Think About" — some questions, a statement, a quiz, a checklist. Though it will take only a minute to work through these little projects, they are important in helping you to see how relevant God's Word is to your life, right now, wherever you are and whatever you do!

2. A Look at Paul's Letter

The Scripture (quoted from the New International Version) is presented first in a grammatical form — actually a *logical* layout. Strict rules of grammar are often bypassed to show logical flow and relationship among various words and phrases. Also, each passage of Scripture presented in this form includes the author's main outline right in the textual material.

3. What Did Paul Say?

A detailed outline follows the Scripture text and appears on the opposite page from the Bible passage. Thus you can read the Scripture first and then get a quick overview of each idea developed in the passage.

4. What Did Paul Mean?

This exposition of the Bible text is the main part of each chapter. The Scripture passage is explained phrase by phrase, verse by verse, and paragraph by paragraph.

5. A Twentieth-Century Application

Though each chapter begins with *you* — as you live in the twentieth century — here you will move from the first century to the twentieth in more depth. After looking at the actual meaning of Paul's words to the Philippians, you will observe how his statements apply in a contemporary situation. In other words, what does this mean to us today? Usually this application is general and relevant to all Christians.

6. A Personal Life Response

We dare not stop with a *general* application, even though it is relevant. What goal or goals can you set for *your* life now to apply this biblical truth? With pencil in hand, you will be encouraged to write out an action step.

7. An Individual or Group Project

This final action is a "follow-through" activity — something to do that will take you even further in understanding what Paul is saying to the Philippians *and* to twentieth century Christians.

Acknowledgments

I would like to express my appreciation to Dr. Donald Campbell, Academic Dean and Professor of Bible Exposition at Dallas Theological Seminary. Dr. Campbell first read this manuscript and offered some very helpful suggestions.

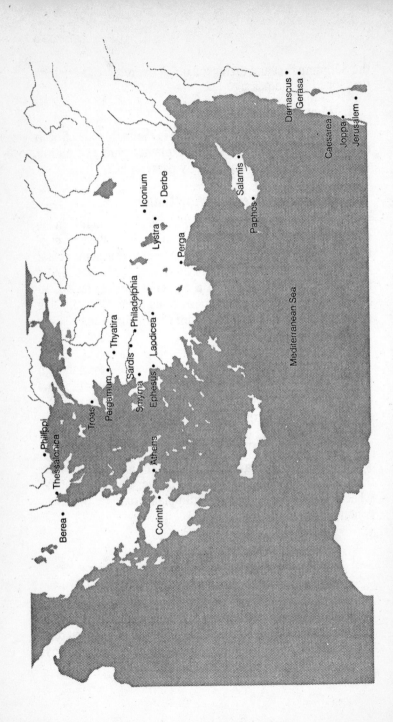

Chapter I

Saints and Servants

SOMETHING TO THINK ABOUT

In evaluating your life, which answers would you check?

	Yes	No	Sometimes	Not Sure
I'm a Saint	☐	☐	☐	☐
I'm a Servant	☐	☐	☐	☐

No matter what your answers, this chapter is designed to help you discover whether you are right or wrong.

A LOOK AT PAUL'S LETTER . . .

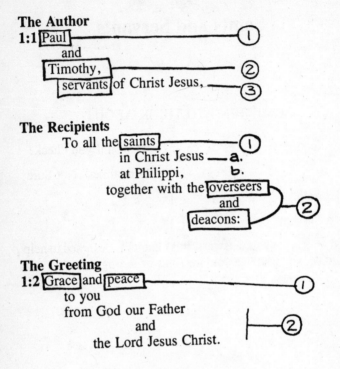

The Author
1:1 Paul
 and
 Timothy,
  servants of Christ Jesus,

The Recipients
 To all the saints
  in Christ Jesus
  at Philippi,
 together with the overseers
  and
 deacons:

The Greeting
1:2 Grace and peace
 to you
 from God our Father
  and
 the Lord Jesus Christ.

WHAT DID PAUL SAY?

A. The Author
1. Paul the apostle

2. Paul's stenographer
3. Their attitude toward Christ

B. The Recipients
1. "All the saints"
   a. Their spiritual position — "in Christ Jesus"
   b. Their earthly position — "at Philippi"
2. The overseers and deacons

C. The Greeting
1. Cultural sensitivity

2. A divine dimension

WHAT DID PAUL MEAN?

The first paragraph in this letter is packed with vital information. We discover the *author*, the *stenographer*, and their attitude toward Jesus Christ. We discover the *recipients*, their position in Christ, where they lived, and that this church was doubtless a well-developed church spiritually and organizationally. We discover a rather common greeting that characterized most letters in this culture, but we also discover why *this greeting* was both common and unique, indicating an unusual relationship between author, stenographer, and the recipients.

A. The Author (1:1)

1. *Paul the Apostle*

Paul was the great apostle to the Gentiles. His letter to the Philippians is one of thirteen that bear his name in the New Testament.

Paul was originally named Saul and was extremely dedicated to pharisaical Judaism. His great pre-conversion accomplishment was to persecute the church — an accomplishment he was later ashamed of when he, too, became a member of the body of Christ and gave his total life to preaching Christ and ministering to people he once tried to imprison and destroy.

When Paul wrote this letter, he was in prison in Rome for the cause of Christ. He had just received a gift — an abundant gift — from the Philippian Christians. They had sent one of their most respected men — a man named Epaphroditus — who delivered their package of love. One of Paul's main purposes in writing this letter was to thank the Philippians for their generosity and concern.

2. *Paul's stenographer*

As Paul wrote this letter, a somewhat younger man no doubt sat at his side with pen in hand — a man Paul had come to love as if he were his very own son. His name was

Timothy. He was probably writing this letter as Paul dictated it.

Timothy had a special place in his heart for the Philippian Christians. And they had a special place in their hearts for him. He had helped start this church. He was with Paul on the second missionary journey when they first came to Philippi. As we'll see later, Timothy's relationship with these Christians was deep and profound. It was fitting that Paul include Timothy in this greeting.

3. *Their attitude toward Christ*

When Paul wrote this letter, he classified both himself and Timothy as "servants of Christ Jesus." The word *servant* literally means a "bond slave." Paul, however, did not use the word *servant* to refer to people who were in *bondage*, but rather to refer to people who were *free*. Paul and Timothy were not serving with a sense of oppression and compulsion, but rather with a sense of privilege and commitment. Both realized with a deep sense of appreciation that Jesus Christ had become *their servant* in order to provide eternal life. Paul especially was grateful to God. After all, he had been an enemy of the cross of Christ. But God, in His love, chose Paul to be one of His choicest servants, in spite of his previous hatred toward Christians and the One they served.

Paul and Timothy, then, had found freedom — not by living for themselves, but by turning their lives over to Christ as His servants. They had truly "lost their lives to find them again" (Mark 8:34-37).

B. The Recipients (1:1)

Paul directed his letter at two groups of Christians. More accurately, there was only *one* group — *all* "the saints." But they also sent a special greeting to a smaller group within the larger group — the church leaders — which he identified as "the overseers and deacons."

1. *"All the saints"*

No word has been more misinterpreted, abused and misused than the word *saint* — both inside and outside the

Christian community. To many, a "saint" is a *special* kind of Christian — one who has lived an unusual life of holiness and dedication.

Not so! A "saint," as Paul used the word, refers to *any* true believer. In fact, *all* the Corinthians were called "saints," and there was a no more carnal group of Christians in all the New Testament world (1 Cor. 1:12; 2 Cor. 1:1,2). A saint, then, is a person "called" and "set apart" by God. The word refers to a man's position "in Christ Jesus." Thus Paul followed this word with the phrase "in Christ Jesus."

a. Their spiritual position — "in Christ Jesus"

To be "in Christ Jesus" is what makes a person a saint. The people Paul was writing to were true believers. They had put their faith in Jesus Christ. They were baptized into one body by the Holy Spirit (1 Cor. 12:13).

Incidentally, the phrase "in Christ Jesus," or a similar one, was one of Paul's favorites. "In Christ Jesus" appears 8 times in the Philippian letter alone, and 41 times in his letters as a whole. The phrase "in Christ" appears 37 times, and "in the Lord" 43 times. Thus this concept appears over 120 times in Paul's writings. To Paul it was a grand and glorious reality to be a Christian — to be "in Christ Jesus."

b. Their earthly position — "at Philippi"

True, Paul was writing to a group of Christians whose citizenship was "in heaven," but they also lived "on earth" — specifically, in Philippi, a significant Roman colony in Macedonia. It was in this city that Paul began his ministry in Europe (see map). He came to Europe as a result of the "Macedonian call" — a vision he had received in the night (Acts 16:8-10). So Paul, Timothy, Silas, and probably Luke packed their bags, crossed the Aegean Sea, and eventually came to Philippi. Here they met a number of people from a variety of backgrounds, led them to Jesus Christ, and established a church that was destined to become one of the most mature groups of Christians in the first century. (The account of the founding of this church is found in Acts 16.)

2. *The overseers (bishops) and deacons*

Within the larger group of Christians at Philippi (the saints) was a smaller group (the church leaders), to whom Paul wished to extend a special greeting. Two interesting observations can be made about the words Paul used to describe these leaders.

a. First, the spiritual leaders at Philippi were called overseers (or bishops) rather than elders, reflecting their cultural background.

Paul used the titles *elder* and *bishop* interchangeably in the New Testament, but with a purpose. The title *elder* was used primarily in churches comprising Christians who were converted in the Jewish culture. The title *overseer* was used in churches that consisted primarily of people who were converted in the Greco-Roman culture. The reason for this is that the word *elder* was a common word among Jews, and the word *overseer* was a common word among the Greeks and Romans. An elder in Israel was a religious and social leader; an overseer in the pagan culture was one who had the oversight of a Roman colony. In both instances, the words were borrowed and given a new meaning and function in the Christian community.

The apostle used the word *overseer* when writing to the Philippians no doubt because the church was heavily populated with Gentile converts. Then, too, many Bible expositors believe that Luke stayed in Philippi to help establish the church when Paul, Timothy, and Silas left to go on to Thessalonica. Since Luke was a Gentile convert, he also may have influenced the Philippians to use the word *overseer* rather than elder.

The overseers at Philippi were those men appointed to *teach* doctrine, *shepherd* the Philippian believers, and *manage* the church of God. These leaders were men mature enough to minister to the spiritual needs of the flock.

b. Second, the fact that Paul greets the ''deacons'' at Philippi indicates that this church was spiritually mature and well developed organizationally.

A deacon in the New Testament was a man appointed to care for the material needs of the body. They seemingly were appointed once a church began to develop and grow and create needs that would not be present when the church was in its infancy. Paul always began in new churches by appointing elders or overseers — for the very first need of any believer is to be taught and to have pastoral care. Thus we see Paul exhorting Titus to appoint elders in Crete — but he said nothing about deacons (Titus 1:5). Evidently the need for deacons had not yet arisen.

Thus the Philippian church was well on its way in its growth and development. They had both overseers *and* deacons — and Paul wanted to greet all the leaders in the church at Philippi in a special way.[1]

C. The Greeting (1:2)

Paul used two words to extend his special greeting — "grace *and* peace." The word *grace* was usually used among Gentiles; the word *peace* was a common greeting among Jews. Consequently Paul uses both — again reflecting his cultural sensitivity.

But Paul adds a divine dimension — a dimension that was noticeably absent in secular correspondence. His greeting was "from God our Father and the Lord Jesus Christ." This gives both *grace* and *peace* a distinctive Christian meaning. Paul was referring to God's unmerited favor and abounding grace toward mankind when He sent Jesus Christ to be the Savior of the world. He was also referring to the peace with God that all men have when they receive God's gift of eternal life.

Thus Paul began his letter with a brief but power-packed paragraph — just two simple verses in our Bible today. These two verses tell us a lot about Paul, Timothy, the Philippians, their church leaders, and the deep relationship that existed between Paul and Timothy and these New Testament Christians.

A TWENTIETH-CENTURY APPLICATION

A. If You Don't Know Christ Personally

Paul refers to the Philippians, the Corinthians, the Ephesians, and the Colossians as "saints." He simply means "believers" or "Christians."

This leads to an important question: What is your relationship with Jesus Christ? Do you know Him personally? If not, you can receive Him right now. This prayer will help you:

"Father, I invite Jesus Christ to be my personal Savior. I am sorry for my sins, and I confess them to You. I need You and believe Jesus died for me personally on the cross and rose again so that I might live forever. Thank You for coming into my life to be my Savior."

B. If You Know Christ Personally

All true Christians are saints, but not all are servants. Have you turned your life over to Jesus Christ totally and unconditionally? Have you come to the point in your life where you have made Him first place? Or are you still running your life — making all your decisions selfishly?

How does a Christian become a servant? First, by making a decision — a decision expressed clearly in Romans 12:1, 2. The following prayer paraphrases that decision:

"Father, in view of all Your mercies and grace to me, I offer myself to You as a living sacrifice, holy and pleasing to You. It is the only reasonable and logical thing for me to do. And from this moment on I will not allow my life to be pressed into this world's pattern and mold, but rather I will become more and more like You through a renewed mind and heart, proving and testing day by day what Your good, pleasing, and perfect will is for my life. In short, Father, I want to be Your servant. I want to lose my life to find it again."

A PERSONAL LIFE RESPONSE

Now that you have made this decision, you must develop a strategy for renewing your mind. Paul sets forth that strategy in Philippians 4:8, 9: "Finally, brothers, whatever is true, whatever is noble, whatever is right, whatever is pure, whatever is lovely, whatever is admirable — if anything is excellent or praiseworthy — think about such things. Whatever you have learned or received or heard from me, or seen in me — put it into practice, and the God of peace will be with you."

Think of one thing in your life that is currently keeping you from serving Jesus Christ with all your heart. The following checklist will help you identify that problem:

Attitude and Actions Toward . . .

☐ My wife   ☐ My husband

☐ My children ☐ My neighbors and friends

☐ Myself   ☐ My work

 ☐ Other _____

My Personal Behavior

☐ In what I read

☐ In what I think about

☐ In what I say to others

☐ In my business ethics

☐ In my eating habits

☐ In my sex life

☐ Other _____

Now write out a goal for this week. Share the goal with someone you really trust and have him pray with you and support you in helping you be a better servant of Jesus Christ.

My goal for this week is _____
_____.

INDIVIDUAL OR GROUP PROJECT

Read Philippians 1:3-11. Answer this question: "What evidence is there in this passage that the Philippian Christians represented a mature church?"

NOTES

[1] For a more extensive development of the concept of elders and deacons and their function in the New Testament church, see *Sharpening the Focus of the Church*, by Gene A. Getz (Chicago: Moody Press, 1975).

Chapter II

A Dynamic Relationship

SOMETHING TO THINK ABOUT

How many Christians can you name with whom you feel you have *deep relationships?*

1. _____

2. _____

3. _____

4. _____

5. _____

If you can name them on one hand, you're probably above normal. If your list is too long, you may *not* know what deep relationships are.

Whatever your response, this chapter will help you discover if you're *normal, abnormal,* or just *uninformed.*

A LOOK AT PAUL'S LETTER . . .

1:3 I thank my God every time I remember you. Ⓐ

1:4 In all my prayers for all of you, Ⓑ
   I always pray with joy

1:5 because of your partnership in the gospel ─①
   from the first day until now,

1:6   being confident of this,
      that He who began a good work in you ─②
         will carry it on to completion
         until the day of Christ Jesus.

1:7 It is right for me to feel this way about all of you,
   since **I have you in my heart;** Ⓒ
   for whether I am in chains
   or
   defending and confirming the gospel,.
      all of you share in God's grace with me.

1:8 God can testify how **I long for all of you**
         with the affection of Christ Jesus. Ⓓ

WHAT DID PAUL SAY?

A. "I thank my God every time I remember you"

B. "I always pray with joy . . ."
1. A continuing and growing relationship

2. A relationship that evidenced reality

C. "I have you in my heart . . ."

D. "I long for all of you . . ."

WHAT DID PAUL MEAN?

There is a key idea that stands out in bold relief in these paragraphs written to the Philippians. It is the idea of *relationships*. Four statements describe Paul's relationships with the Philippian Christians; these statements, in turn, form the basic points that will be developed in this chapter.

A. "I thank my God every time I remember you" (1:3)

This passage teaches that *close human relationships* and *the motivation to pray* are intricately interwoven. In fact, prayer becomes meaningful in the context of human relationships.

Paul demonstrated this truth dramatically in his letter to the Philippian Christians. His prayers of thanksgiving were prompted by pleasant *memories* — memories of *people* he knew and loved.

For most of us memories fade. Even the most sensitive relationships are soon forgotten. Think about that for a moment. Think of your childhood relationships — the friends you thought you'd never forget! Think of your youth — the buddies you played with, the girls or fellows you dated!

Some of you have moved from one locality to another in the last several years, leaving friends and relatives you thought you could never live without. Yet here you are! How much do you miss them now? Some of them — why, you've even forgotten their names.

How quickly we forget. How quickly the memories of tears shed in parting fade into the past. How quickly even those who have had a gigantic impact upon our lives — such as parents — become a memory so faded that we can't recall the reasons they were once so meaningful to us in years gone by.

Such is the tragedy of many human relationships, even among Christians. Sadly, Christian relationships can be shallow and superficial.

Not so with Paul and his relationship to the Philippian

Christians — and they with him. *Every time he remembered them – he thanked God for them*. But there was a reason. The context of Paul's statement, as we will see, spells out why.

B. "I always pray with joy . . ." (1:4)

Every time Paul remembered the Philippian Christians *he thanked God for them!* And every time he thanked God for them, it was a prayer of *joy*. In other words, his memories were positive; consequently his prayers, too, were happy experiences. Not only is the motivation to pray related to the quality of human relationships, but the more significant the relationships, the more exciting the prayer experience.

Paul's motivation to pray for the Philippians was based on two factors: first, the continuing and growing relationship they had with each other (1:5); second, the evidence this relationship produced regarding the reality of their Christian experience (1:6).

1. *A continuing and growing relationship*

"I always pray with joy," said Paul, "because of your partnership in the gospel from the first day until now. . . ."

From the very first moment that Paul succeeded in winning someone to Jesus Christ in Philippi, he experienced an eager and cooperative spirit in the work of the gospel (Acts 16:13-15). Lydia, a saleslady of purple garments, and a proselyte to Judaism, responded first to the gospel. Then her whole household became Christians.

But probably the most memorable event in Paul's relationship with Lydia was when she insisted that Paul and his fellow missionaries (Silas, Timothy, and Luke) stay in her home — using it as a base for their spiritual operations (Acts 16:15). It may also be that her home became the first meeting place for the new believers in Philippi.

Paul remembered this event and possibly was referring to it when he wrote that he prayed "with joy" because of their "partnership in the gospel from the *first day*" (1:5).

Yet Paul specifies that this "partnership in the gospel" was "from the first day until *now*." The relationship and fellowship in the gospel which began in Lydia's home in the early days of the Philippian church was an *ongoing* experience. Again and again, after Paul had left Philippi to start new churches, these Christians had sent gifts to meet Paul's material needs (4:15, 16). And now, once again, they had sent a gift to him while he was in a Roman prison. Epaphroditus, perhaps an elder or overseer in the church at Philippi, had delivered the gift, almost losing his life in the process (2:29, 30).

Epaphroditus returned to Philippi carrying Paul's letter, written with deep feeling and meaning: "I always pray with joy because of your partnership in the gospel from the first day until now" (1:5).

2. *A relationship that evidenced reality*

Paul's motivation to pray for these Christians was also based on this second factor, which grows naturally out of the first. The aging apostle was very confident that the salvation experience of the Philippians was real and truly a work of God in their hearts. His prayers of thanksgiving for these Christians were also prayers of joy because he was confident that God, "who began a good work" in these people, would "carry it on to completion" until the day Christ came again (1:6).

This "good work" Paul referred to was doubtless, first of all, God's work of redemption in their own hearts — making them new creatures in Christ (2 Cor. 5:17). More specifically, Paul is probably referring to the "good work" of participating in the work of redemption and reconciliation on behalf of others (2 Cor. 5:18-21). With every gift they gave to support Paul's work they were sharing in the fulfillment of the Great Commission of our Lord (Matt. 28:19, 20; Phil. 4:17).

C. "I have you in my heart . . ." (1:7)

This next statement of Paul indicates even more fully how close he felt to the Philippians spiritually and emotionally.

Though absent physically from them, he sensed a oneness in Christ that went beyond any explanation. In Christ, the "unity of the Spirit" and the experience of being "one body in Christ" with these believers was not destroyed by distance.

Thus Paul understood *why* he felt so close to these people. "It is right," he said, "for me to feel this way about all of you, since I have you in my heart." In other words, Paul said that "you Philippians are one with me . . . I sense it . . . I feel it . . . I know it by experience — even though you are miles away."

Paul then gave more specific testimony as to why this relationship exists: "for whether I am in chains [bound to a Roman guard] or defending and confirming the gospel [preaching the gospel in the midst of opposition], all of you share in God's grace with me" (1:7). Paul seemed to sense — though at a distance — that the Philippians were "standing right beside him" sharing in the experience of God's marvelous grace, enabling him to fulfill his mission in this world in spite of difficult circumstances.

They too were suffering for Christ, and Paul was aware of their suffering. Thus Paul said later in this letter: "For it has been granted to you on behalf of Christ not only to believe on him, but also to suffer for him, since you are going through the same struggle you saw I had, and now hear that I still have" (1:29, 30). Both Paul and the Philippians, then, were sharing together in God's grace that enabled them to be true to their calling in Christ.

D. "I long for all of you . . ." (1:8)

Though Paul experienced even at a distance the very oneness and "presence" of the Philippians, it was no substitute for face-to-face fellowship. The apostle was a human being like you and me. He was lonely, and his heart yearned to see the Philippians and to add to their progress and joy in the faith (2:24). The love that possessed his total being was the very love of Christ that had been poured into his heart by the Holy

Spirit (1:8; Rom. 5:5). Though he was not a superhuman being, he was controlled by a supernatural God who enabled him to love others in a supernatural way.

A TWENTIETH-CENTURY APPLICATION

A. Some Observations

1. Prayer, to be meaningful and exciting, must involve a human as well as a divine dimension. It must be both horizontal and vertical. It must grow out of deep human relationships with other believers. This, of course, is the context of much of Paul's prayer life (Rom. 1:8; 1 Cor. 1:4; Eph. 4:15-19), as well as his and other New Testament writers' instructions to others regarding prayer (Rom. 12:10-13; 1 Thess. 5:14-18; James 5:13-16; 1 Peter 4:7-10).

2. Human relationships do not just happen — even in Christ. They must be carefully cultivated and maintained. For example, the Philippians worked hard at expressing their love and concern to Paul. They kept communication lines open. Paul in turn did the same.

B. Some Questions to Think About

1. How many Christians can you name with whom you feel you have deep relationships?
2. How many people do you know who cause you spontaneously to thank God for them when you remember them?
3. When you pray for a brother or sister in Christ, do you ever experience *joy* because of your partnership with them in the work of Christ?
4. Do you know of any Christians who cause you joy because of their progress in Christ?
5. How diligent are you about cultivating and maintaining relationships with other Christians? Do you wait for others to take the initiative — and then complain that no one really cares about you?
6. What about people you "used to know"? How well have you kept communication lines open?

7. Do you even want to get to know others beyond a superficial level?

A PERSONAL LIFE RESPONSE

In light of the above questions, what do you believe is the most significant need in your own life for building better Christian relationships? Perhaps you need to begin with your husband or wife. Or your children. What about your parents? What about a brother or sister in Christ who is lonely, needy, or neglected? Perhaps you need to begin with yourself — your *insecurity* or your *selfishness* or your *priorities*.

Take a moment to write down *one* goal that will help you build better and deeper relationships with other believers.

My goal, beginning this week, is to _____
_____.

INDIVIDUAL OR GROUP PROJECT

Read once again Philippians 1:9-11. How does this paragraph relate to Paul's statement in 1 Corinthians 13:13?

Chapter III
Paul's Prayer

SOMETHING TO THINK ABOUT

From what you already know about the Philippian Christians, how would you rank their maturity level as a body of New Testament believers?

☐ Very mature

☐ About average

☐ Average

☐ Immature

☐ Very immature

Let's look at Paul's prayer for the Philippians. It will show you how Paul would have answered this question.

1:9 And this is my prayer:
    that your (love) may abound (more) and (more)
          in knowledge   ①
          and
          depth of insight, —— ②

1:10   **so that you may be able to discern what is best**
        and
        may be pure and blameless
            until the day of Christ,
1:11   **filled with the fruit of righteousness**
     ① —— that comes through Jesus Christ
     ② —— to the glory and praise of God.

WHAT DID PAUL SAY?

A. "That Your LOVE may abound MORE and MORE"
   1. In knowledge

   2. In depth of insight

B. "That you may be able to discern what is best"

C. That you "may be pure and blameless"

D. "Filled with the fruit of righteousness"
   1. The source — Jesus Christ
   2. The purpose — the glory and praise of God

WHAT DID PAUL MEAN?

In the paragraphs of Philippians described in chapter 2, Paul shared with the Christians his *attitude* and *feelings* toward them when he remembered them and *prayed* for them — an attitude and feeling of thankfulness, joy, confidence, longing, and affection. And now, in this paragraph (vv. 9-11), Paul specified the *content* of his prayer.

A. "That your love may abound more and more" (1:9)

Paul made clear in his correspondence what he believed were the marks of a mature church. For example, after a lengthy discussion of spiritual gifts in his Corinthian letter, he succinctly summarized what were the *most important* manifestations of maturity in a body of believers. "And now these three remain: *faith, hope* and *love*. But," said Paul, "the greatest of these is *love*" (1 Cor. 13:13).

Paul was consistent about this concept. Note the introductory paragraphs in his letters to other New Testament churches, observing particularly what Paul thanked God for.

To the Thessalonian Christians he wrote:

"We always thank God for all of you, mentioning you in our prayers. We continually remember before our God and Father your work produced by *faith,* your labor prompted by *love,* and your endurance inspired by *hope* in our Lord Jesus Christ" (1 Thess. 1:2, 3).

"We ought always to thank God for you, brothers, and rightly so, because your *faith* is growing more and more, and the *love* every one of you has for each other is increasing. Therefore, among God's churches we boast about your perseverence and faith in all the persecutions and trials you are enduring" (2 Thess. 1:3, 4).

Paul wrote to the Colossian Christians and the Ephesian Christians, and we see a similar pattern in his introductory paragraphs:

"We always thank God, the Father of our Lord Jesus

Christ, when we pray for you, because we have heard of your *faith* in Christ Jesus and of the *love* you have for all the saints — the *faith* and *love* that spring from the *hope* stored up for you in heaven, and which you have already heard about in the word of truth, the gospel that has come to you" (Col. 1:3-6).

"For this reason, I, since I heard about your *faith* in the Lord Jesus and your *love* for all the saints, have never stopped giving thanks for you, remembering you in my prayers" (Eph. 1:15).

In all these paragraphs Paul "thanks God" for the manifestation of these qualities of faith, hope, and love — *especially love*. Note his statement to the Colossians: "And over all these virtues put on *love,* which binds them all together in perfect unity" (Col. 3:14).

There is no doubt, then, what Paul believed were the marks of a mature body of believers. Love was the all-encompassing virtue; it was the greatest.

You may ask, Why this extensive elaboration on the concepts of *faith, hope,* and *love?* Because we cannot comprehend fully Paul's prayer for the Philippians without understanding the larger context of his thinking. Observe again that Paul prayed that their "love may abound more and more." Thus Paul acknowledged, first of all, the love that already existed in the Philippian body. There was much evidence of that. Had they not demonstrated it again and again in their concern for Paul?

Second, Paul encouraged the constant development of this love, again demonstrating that growing toward maturity is a continuing process while we are yet on this earth (Eph. 4:15, 16).

There is a third observation that emerges from seeing Paul's prayer for the Philippians in the larger context of faith, hope, and love. Significantly Paul mentions *only love* when he prayed for the Philippian Christians. Thus Paul seems to imply that the Philippians — of all the New Testament churches — were already demonstrating the "most excellent way . . . the way of love" (1 Cor. 12:31; 14:1). Furthermore

Paul in his great love chapter (1 Cor. 13) also implies that the "way of love" in its mature manifestation includes *faith* and *hope*. Love, said Paul, "always trusts" and "always hopes" (1 Cor. 13:7). Where there is *mature love,* there is always *faith* and *hope.*

1. *"In knowledge"*

Note that Paul prayed that the Philippians' "love may abound more and more *in knowledge.*" Again we see a correlation between Paul's prayer for the Philippians and his admonitions to the Corinthians.

In 1 Corinthians 13 — after graphically demonstrating to the Corinthians their lack of love — Paul reminded them that certain gifts will pass away. But, he said, "When perfection [or maturity] comes, the imperfect [or the state of immaturity] disappears" (v. 10). Paul then compared this process with natural growth from childhood to adulthood: "When I was a child, I talked like a child, I thought like a child, I reasoned like a child. When I became a man, I put childish ways behind me" (v. 11).

The most important correlation between the Philippian prayer and the Corinthian exhortation comes in 1 Corinthians 13:12: "Now we see but a poor reflection; then we shall see face to face. Now I know in part; then I shall *know fully.* ..."

The Greek word translated *know fully* in 13:12 is the same basic word *(epiginōskō)* translated *knowledge* in Philippians 1:9 — meaning full and complete and experiential knowledge. Thus Paul's prayer was that the Philippian Christians' "love may abound more and more in *knowledge"* – that is, in a complete, full, and experiential knowledge of God as revealed in Jesus Christ and His Word.

When Paul wrote to the Corinthians, he referred to the same concept again, only in different words: "And we," he wrote, "who with unveiled faces all reflect the Lord's glory, are being transformed into His likeness with ever-increasing glory, which comes from the Lord, who is the Spirit" (2 Cor. 3:18). In other words, Christian maturity in a local body of believers reflects the image of God, and since "God is love," the most significant mark of Christian maturity is love — an ever-increasing and abounding love (Phil. 1:9).

2. *"In depth of insight"*

Paul prayed that their "love may abound more and more in knowledge and *depth of insight.*"

"Experiential knowledge" can hardly be separated from "depth of insight." A maturing knowledge of God Himself enables a Christian to function wisely and with good judgment — making proper decisions. This leads to a second part of Paul's prayer, which grows naturally out of his initial request to God on behalf of the Philippians.

B. "That you may be able to discern what is best" (1:10)

An "experiential knowledge" of God and "depth of insight" enable believers, both individually and as a body, to discern the will of God. The Greek word translated *discern* in Philippians 1:10 is the same basic word *(dokimadzein)* translated *test and approve* in Romans 12:2, which reads: "Do not conform any longer to the pattern of this world, but be transformed by the renewing of your mind. Then you will be able to *test* and *approve* [discern] what God's will is — his good, pleasing and perfect will." An experiential knowledge of God and depth of insight enable a body of Christians to discern the mind of God relative to their life on this earth.

C. That you "may be pure and blameless" (1:10)

As "depth of insight" is inseparably linked to "an experiential knowledge of God," so a "pure and blameless life" is inseparably linked to being able to "discern what is best." Paul interrelates these concepts in Romans 12:1,2 as well, for he exhorted the Roman Christians to offer themselves "as living sacrifices, holy and pleasing to God." They were not to "conform any longer to the pattern of the world," which the apostle John defined as "the cravings of sinful man, the lust of his eyes and his pride in possessions" (1 John 2:15,

16). This, of course, is what Paul was also praying for the Philippians — that they "may be pure and blameless."

D. "Filled with the fruit of righteousness that comes through Jesus Christ — to the glory and praise of God" (1:11)

Paul summed up his prayer by referring to the *source* of all he prayed for in the lives of the Philippian Christians as well as His *purpose*.

1. *The source – Jesus Christ*

In essence, the fruit of righteousness is *love*, and so are its corresponding characteristics: experiential knowledge, depth of insight, discernment, and a pure and blameless life. The source of this righteousness is Jesus Christ Himself — through His death and resurrection. He provides not only the image, the goal, and the standard, but also the inner strength and power to live a life of abounding love. Thus Paul exhorted the Ephesian Christians to "be strong in the Lord and in his mighty power" (Eph. 6:10).

2. *The purpose – the glory and praise of God*

To live a life wholly for God is not for the purpose of personal benefit, though there certainly is personal reward and blessing. Rather, Paul reminded the Christians at Philippi that a life of love will become an occasion for manifesting God's glory and bringing praise to the Lord Jesus Christ.

This is why God chose us and redeemed us in the first place. Three times in the first chapter of the Ephesian letter, Paul drove home this point: "In love he predestined us . . . to the *praise of His glorious grace*. . . . In him [Christ] we were also chosen . . . in order that we . . . might be for the *praise of his glory*. . . . In him . . . you were marked with a seal, the promised Holy Spirit . . . to the *praise of His* [God's] *glory*" (1:5, 6, 11-14).

A TWENTIETH-CENTURY APPLICATION

The greatest need in today's churches is for believers as a

body to manifest to all people faith, hope, and love — above all, love which creates unity. Jesus said: "A new commandment I give you: Love one another. As I have loved you, so you must love one another. All men will know that you are my disciples if you love one another" (John 13:34, 35).

Satan's greatest attack throughout church history — from New Testament times until today — has been to sidetrack Christians onto peripheral issues, creating disunity, bickering, selfishness, and pride. When Satan achieves this goal, he has broken down the greatest bridge to the world — the bridge of love.

In many good Bible-teaching churches today, there is another problem. We are often strong on theology and doctrine, but weak on relationships within the body. It is obvious from the Philippian letter that these New Testament Christians were strong in *both* areas. They were well-grounded in the Scriptures, and they had a profound love and concern for one another.

There are two questions every local church in the twentieth century needs to ask and answer in order to pinpoint problems that may be keeping true Christian love from developing:

1. Do we have a balanced emphasis on learning Scripture *and* experiencing vital relationships with other members of the body?
2. Do our church structures and forms help create an atmosphere of warmth and openness in the body, or do they encourage people to remain aloof and alone?

In some churches, people sit side by side every Sunday, but never get to know other Christians intimately. They learn lots of Bible truth, but never learn to express that truth in dynamic Christian relationships. An analysis of their church forms frequently reveals that the way the church is organized encourages "distance" rather than "closeness" among members of the body of Christ.

How do your church forms and structures measure up?

A PERSONAL LIFE RESPONSE

When all is said and done, we must get very personal about these matters. As an individual, you need to respond to the Word of God. How do you evaluate your life as a Christian today as compared with a year ago? Have *you* grown in *your* love for God and for others? In what ways have you contributed to the spiritual maturity of the body of believers with whom you fellowship?

Write down at least three concrete evidences of your spiritual growth:

1. _____

2. _____

3. _____

INDIVIDUAL OR GROUP PROJECT

Review this chapter with your family or a group of believers. Discuss the answers to these questions: How do we as a family or group measure up to the standard of love set forth in the Bible (see 1 Cor. 13:4-7)? What factors are keeping us from being a mature Christian group?

Remember: An ideal for the Christian family is to be a mature and functioning church in miniature.

Chapter IV

Paul's Attitude Toward Suffering

SOMETHING TO THINK ABOUT

Why do Christians suffer? Why have *you* suffered?

These are profound questions, and legitimate ones. Many people have asked these same questions for centuries.

The Bible has much to say about suffering and why it happens. In fact, Paul spoke about this subject on many occasions. In his letter to the Philippians, he wrote about his *own* suffering and about what happened because of it.

A LOOK AT PAUL'S LETTER . . .

The purpose Paul sees in his suffering
1:12 Now I want you to know, brothers,
      that what has happened to me
        has really served
              to advance the gospel

The ways the gospel was advanced
1:13 As a result,
      it has become clear throughout the whole palace
      guard and to everyone else
      that I am in chains for Christ.

      1:14 Because of my chains,
        most of the brothers in the Lord
          have been encouraged to speak the word
        of God
        more courageously and fearlessly.

1:15 It is true that some preach out of envy and rivalry, ③
      but others out of good will.

1:16 The latter do so in love, knowing
      that I am put here for the defense of the gospel.

1:17 The former preach out of selfish ambition, not sin-
      cerely,
      supposing that they can stir up trouble for me while I
        am in chains.

Paul's attitude in the midst of suffering
1:18 But what does it matter?
      The important thing is that in every way,
        whether from false motives or true,
        Christ is preached.
      And because of this I rejoice.

Other reasons why Christians suffer

WHAT DID PAUL SAY?

A. The purpose Paul sees in his suffering

B. The ways the gospel was advanced

    1. In the pagan community

    2. In the Christian community

    3. In the Jewish community

C. Paul's attitude in the midst of suffering

D. Other reasons why Christians suffer

WHAT DID PAUL MEAN?

A. The purpose Paul sees in his suffering — to advance the gospel (1:12)

The Philippian Christians had been extremely concerned about Paul's situation in Rome. No doubt one of the burning questions they had when Epaphroditus had left to search him out related to his physical condition. And as he penned a letter — soon to be carried by Epaphroditus to them — he spoke to their question about his welfare: "Now I want you to know, brothers," he said, "that what has happened to me has really served to *advance* the gospel" (1:12).

Paul was a prisoner when he wrote this letter. No doubt he penned this epistle to the Philippians sometime during the two-year period he stayed in his own rented quarters, chained to a Roman guard (Acts 28:16, 30).[1]

But note the purpose Paul saw in his imprisonment and consequent suffering. "I'm alive and well," he wrote. "True, I'm in chains and I have had a rough time, but the important thing is that *people are finding out about Jesus Christ.*"

What a fantastic attitude! Paul had a marvelous capacity to see a *positive purpose* in all that happened to him. He could have folded his hands and for two long, agonizing years wallowed in self-pity.

Not Paul. He saw a golden opportunity. Three days after he settled into his quarters, "he called together the leaders of the Jews" (Acts 28:17). When they arrived, he reviewed the circumstances leading to his present condition (vv. 17-20). He found an openness at least to hear his viewpoint, and on subsequent days the Jewish leaders returned to hear Paul explain the Old Testament and how Jesus Christ — the hope of Israel — had already come.

Some believed Paul. But others rejected his message. And this was the beginning of a marvelous evangelistic effort that spread out from Paul's prison home.

B. The ways in which the gospel was advanced (1:13-17)

How long Paul had been in bonds when he wrote this letter we do not know, but it was long enough to have a strong impact on the city of Rome — and probably beyond. His clear testimony for Jesus Christ affected numerous people from all walks of life.[2]

1. *The pagan community*

When illustrating how the gospel had been advanced as a result of his imprisonment, Paul referred first to the pagan community — actually the last group he ministered to directly. "As a result," he wrote, "it has become clear *throughout the whole palace guard* . . . that I am in chains for Christ" (Phil. 1:13).

When the Jewish leaders first came to hear Paul explain why he was in prison in Rome, numerous pagan guards who stood by Paul's side twenty-four hours a day heard his story again and again. As Luke reported, "For two whole years Paul stayed there in his own rented house and welcomed all who came to see him. Boldly and without hindrance he preached the kingdom of God and taught about the Lord Jesus Christ" (Acts 28:30, 31).

History records that there were about nine thousand men who comprised the imperial bodyguard in Rome. It is hard to imagine that a majority of these men heard about Paul's imprisonment, but yet not impossible. Paul was a special case. To our knowledge, no one earlier had been "in chains for Christ." For robbery, murder, and other crimes, yes; but not for following a religious man who claimed to be God.

This was something unusual. No doubt there was much talk about this strange little Jew who was stirring up the Jewish community with his teaching. No doubt guard after guard walked away from his turn at Paul's side, scratching his head and wondering what it was all about. Eventually, one by one many of the guards themselves probably became Christians.

But Paul's unique imprisonment was talked about by more people than the guards themselves. "It has become clear . . . to *everyone else*," wrote Paul, "that I am in chains for Christ" (1:13). Soon large numbers of people scattered all over the city found out about Paul. The name of Christ became a common topic of conversation. "Who *is* this Christ?" would be the natural question. "He must be an unusual person to command such loyalty," would be the logical conclusion. "Let's find out more!" would be the natural response.

It is conceivable that the guards themselves coveted the opportunity to guard Paul — just to add variety and interest to what ordinarily would be a boring task.

Paul was excited with these opportunities to share Christ with the pagan world. After all, this was his primary goal in life. When many of the Jews would not respond to the gospel, Luke reported, Paul turned once again to the Gentiles and preached the gospel to them (Acts 28:25-30). Beginning with the Roman guards, he then had opportunity to share Christ with many Roman citizens who came — possibly out of curiosity — to hear Paul preach the gospel (v. 30).

2. *The Christian community*

Paul's imprisonment also encouraged the other Christians in Rome to talk about Jesus Christ. When they saw Paul's boldness, they began to "speak the word of God more courageously and fearlessly" (1:14).

Something within man responds to bravery in others. I remember visiting the Alamo in San Antonio, Texas. There a small band of men knew their destiny was sealed if they stayed to fight the large encampment of Mexican soldiers who were about to advance on the small mission church that was their only refuge. Col. W. B. Travis drew a line in the dust with his sword, challenging the men to step across who would stay and fight to death. Every man but one responded to the challenge — even Col. James Bowie, who lay wounded on a cot.

"Carry me across the line," Bowie shouted to his comrades.

Every man was killed — including Bowie, who fought off the enemy as best he could from his deathbed.

All true Americans "remember the Alamo." But often as Christians we do not remember the Christians who suffered and even died for their faith in Jesus Christ.

There were many Christians in Rome who saw Paul's boldness — even while chained to a Roman guard — and they drew strength from his dynamic life and witness. If a man who was in prison could speak clearly for Christ, what about people who were free?

3. *The Jewish community*

There are many opinions as to what Paul was referring to in 1:15-17, when he wrote about those who preached Christ "out of envy and rivalry . . . out of selfish ambition, not sincerely, supposing that they can stir up trouble" for Paul while he was in chains. Who were these people with false motives?

Some believe these were Judaizers — those "Christians" who mixed law and grace. But on other occasions Paul was emphatic about his displeasure when a "false gospel" was preached (Gal. 1:6-9). Thus for Paul to condone the activity of Judaizers in Rome does not seem to correspond with his attitude on other occasions.

Others believe he was referring to Christians who had "false motives" in setting out to cause persecution for Paul. Yet it is hard to envision Christians who would increase the suffering of the very one who first communicated to them the message of freedom in Christ.

Another point of view is feasible and, in fact, seems to make more sense. Again, a careful study of Luke's account in Acts 16, as compared with Philippians 1:12-18, seems to support the idea that these people were *unconverted Jews*.

Note that Paul first called for the Jewish leaders to come to his prison home to hear him interpret the Old Testament. From morning until evening Paul "explained and declared to them the kingdom of God and tried to convince them about Jesus from the Law of Moses and from the Prophets'' (Acts 28:23). Some were persuaded that Jesus Christ was the true Messiah; but others "would not believe." In fact, "they disagreed among themselves and began to leave."

This event in the life of the Jewish community evidently set off a heated discussion among their leaders. With the growing number of Gentiles who began to respond to the gospel, they were probably soon involved in a massive smear campaign against Paul.

But they had to meet Paul on his terms — Jesus Christ! Was He or was He not the true Messiah? This was the debate. And so in "reverse fashion" the Jews who did not believe that Jesus was the Christ actually became instruments that helped demonstrate that He *was* the Christ; in their "envy and rivalry," their "selfish ambition" and their "false motives," they actually "preached Christ" as they tried to discredit Him.

This was not a new phenomenon among unbelieving Israel. It happened when Jesus Christ was on earth. John recorded for us the story of the man born blind who actually *came to faith in Christ* because of the Jewish arguments *against* Christ (John 9). So it seems that the more these Jewish leaders in Rome tried to convince people that Jesus was not the Christ, the more people were convinced that He was!

C. Paul's attitude in the midst of his suffering (1:18)

Paul ends this dynamic paragraph in his letter to the Philippian Christians with these words: "But what does it matter? The important thing is that in every way, whether from false motives or true, Christ is preached. And because of this *I rejoice*."

The gospel was advancing, and Paul saw this positive purpose in his suffering. Perhaps he saw more evangelistic results in this two-year period than in any other period of his life. How could he be sad and depressed when the very purpose for which he was born was being fulfilled in a remarkable way?

D. Other reasons why Christians suffer

Various purposes can be accomplished when Christians suffer.

1. *To communicate the gospel of Christ*

In this instance, suffering helped Paul communicate the message of life in Christ. This gave Paul hope and joy during his imprisonment.

2. *To understand the sufferings of others*

On other occasions, Paul understood that his own suffering would help him empathize with others in distress. In turn, he could minister more effectively to those in trouble, sharing with them the same comfort he had "received from God" (2 Cor. 1:3-5).

3. *To produce Christian maturity*

James reminded Christians that suffering, when viewed properly, can produce maturity. "Consider it pure joy, my brothers, whenever you face trials of many kinds, because you know that the testing of your faith develops perseverance. Perseverance must finish its work so that you may be mature and complete, not lacking anything" (James 1:2-4).

4. *Because of personal sin*

The writer of the Book of Hebrews reminds us that Christians sometimes suffer because of sin in their lives. If we are His sons and are "naughty," God, as a loving Father, disciplines us — not to punish us, but lovingly to bring us back into fellowship with Him (12:5-10). "No discipline seems pleasant at the time, but painful. Later on, however, it produces a harvest of righteousness and peace for those who have been trained by it" (12:11).

5. *Because we live in a world contaminated by sin*

There is also suffering that results from the fact that we live in a world polluted by sin. It sometimes happens because of other people and is thus beyond our control. For example, insensitive and selfish parents sometimes create problems for their children, causing much emotional and even physical distress.

6. *Suffering we cannot understand*

There is also a kind of suffering we cannot understand at all. It is difficult to see a reason, let alone a purpose. Job had this kind of experience. Yet he trusted God even when all others had turned away from him — even his wife, who advised him to "curse God and die."

But because Job knew God in a personal way, he also knew that beyond this life he would understand. He saw "meaning" in his suffering, even though it had to be based on the fact that God is a God who ultimately will make all things clear (Rom. 8:28).

7. *To bring an individual to a salvation experience*

Suffering has also been the occasion for some persons' inviting Jesus Christ to be their Savior. Without coming to the place of helplessness, they may never have turned to God for help. Better to suffer in this life than to spend all eternity separated from God!

A TWENTIETH-CENTURY APPLICATION

What is my attitude toward suffering? Do I try to develop a positive attitude toward the experience, no matter what its cause? Or do I spend most of my time feeling sorry for myself or being bitter toward God and others? Do I look for opportunities to turn a burden into a blessing? Do I try by faith to see some meaning in the experience, even if I can't understand clearly *why* the problem exists, or what its specific purpose is?

A PERSONAL LIFE RESPONSE

Select one circumstance in your own life that is a burden. What possible meaning can you see in this experience that will enable you to be a more mature Christian? How can you turn this negative situation into a positive experience — either for yourself or in the life of someone else. Be specific. What step will you take first?

INDIVIDUAL OR GROUP PROJECT

Together as a group (your family, for example) or as an individual determine how you can help someone who is in distress. What can you do to ease his burden and to help him find happiness in the midst of the problem?

NOTES

[1] It is recognized that there are several viewpoints regarding *where* and *when* Paul was in prison. Some believe — and on some good evidence — that he was imprisoned in Ephesus. But the point of view of this author is that he was in Rome and that it was during the two-year period he was in his own rented quarters. Although in chains, he was given freedom to communicate the gospel. It seems that the textual material itself in Philippians 1:12-18, when carefully correlated with Acts 28:16-30, supports this hypothesis.

[2] All evidence in the Philippian passage seems to point to the fact that when Paul wrote this, he had been confined for a substantial period of time — perhaps most of the two-year period.

Chapter V

Paul's Philosophy of Life

SOMETHING TO THINK ABOUT

If you were totally honest, what word or words would you put in the blank in response to this multiple-choice question?

FOR TO ME, TO LIVE IS_____!

a. Money   e. My home   i. Sex

b. Entertainment f. My family   j. My work

c. Friends   g. Myself   k. Sports

d. School   h. Fun   l. Other ____

How would Paul have answered this question? He leaves no room for speculation in his Philippian letter.

A LOOK AT PAUL'S LETTER . . .

Paul's Hope

1:18b Yes, and I will continue to rejoice,

1:19 for I know that through your prayers and the help
given by the Spirit of Jesus Christ,
what has happened to me

Source

will turn out for my deliverance.

1:20 I eagerly expect and hope that I will in no way be
ashamed,
but will have sufficient courage
so that now as always Christ will be
exalted
in my body,
whether by life or by death.

Paul's Struggle

1:21 For to me, to live is Christ ①
and to die is gain. ②

1:22 If I am to go on living in the body,
this will mean fruitful labor for me.
Yet, what shall I choose? I do not know!

1:23 I am torn between the two:
I desire to depart and be with Christ,
which is better by far;

Paul's Decision

1:24 but, it is more necessary for you that I remain in the
body.

1:25 Convinced of this, I know that I will remain, — ①
and I will continue with all of you — ②
for your progress and joy in the faith,

1:26 so that through my being with you again
your joy in Christ Jesus will
overflow on account of me.

WHAT DID PAUL SAY?

A. Paul's Hope
1. His source of hope
   a. The prayers of the Philippians
   b. The Holy Spirit
   c. God's faithfulness in the past

2. His hope explained
   a. I will be delivered
   b. I will not be ashamed
   c. I will have sufficient courage
   d. I will exalt Christ in my body

B. Paul's Struggle
1. To live is Christ
2. To die is gain

C. Paul's Decision

1. I will remain

2. I will minister to you

WHAT DID PAUL MEAN?

A. Paul's Hope (1:18b-20)

Hope was one of Paul's favorite words. As we have observed, he used it to describe Christian maturity. When writing to the New Testament churches, he often thanked God for their faith, *hope,* and love (Col. 1:3-5; 1 Thess. 1:2, 3).

When Paul spoke of hope in this instance, he was not using the word to express uncertainty. When someone asks you if you are going to do something, you might reply, "I hope so!" This is not what Paul meant. To him, a Christian's *hope* was a reality — a certainty! He spoke of hope that is "firm" and a hope that is "good" (2 Cor. 1:7; 2 Thess. 2:16).

And so again, when he wrote to the Philippians he wrote with *assurance:* "I eagerly expect and *hope* that I will in no way be ashamed." Paul was sure that no matter what happened to him personally, he would win.

In this passage Paul first spoke of the *source* of this hope and second *explained more fully* what his hope really was.

1. *His source of hope*

Paul's hope for deliverance from his present situation was based on three factors: the prayers of the Philippian Christians, the Holy Spirit, and his previous experience with Jesus Christ.

a. The prayers of the Philippians

The Philippians had been his partners in the ministry from the very beginning of their association together as brothers and sisters in Jesus Christ (1:5). Part of that partnership very likely involved intercessory prayer. Paul was convinced that these Christians would continue to pray for him right up to the time when Christ came again (1:6.)[1]

Paul also believed in the *power* of prayer. It was no mere religious ritual. "For I *know,*" he said with assurance, "that *through your prayers* . . . what has happened to me will turn out for my deliverance" (1:19).

b. The Holy Spirit

Paul had a second source of hope — ''the help given by the Spirit of Jesus Christ.'' He was one of those select New Testament saints who received direct communication from God. The very letter he was writing resulted from special revelation. Inspired by the Holy Spirit, he penned an epistle that was directly from God Himself (2 Tim. 3:16, 17).

From his conversion onward (Acts 9:3-19), however, Paul had many direct experiences with God. The Holy Spirit spoke expressly to the Christians at Antioch when Paul was first commissioned to preach the gospel (Acts 13:2). By direct revelation Paul was given power to ''see right through'' Elymas the sorcerer (Acts 13:8-12). Through direct communication from the Holy Spirit, Paul was stopped from preaching the gospel in Asia and was redirected to the country where the Philippians resided — Macedonia (Acts 16:6-10). In fact, by direct revelation from the Spirit — through the prophet Agabus — Paul was warned of the very imprisonment he was now experiencing (Acts 21:10, 11).

The Holy Spirit was not a stranger to Paul. Now bound in chains, as the Holy Spirit had predicted, Paul was confident that he would receive help from ''the Spirit of Jesus Christ'' to face whatever lay ahead (1:19). This help probably came in the form of utterance and the ability to make a clearcut and courageous defense before those who would try him. Jesus Christ had made a marvelous promise to several of His apostles which was also applicable to Paul: ''Whenever you are arrested and brought to trial, do not worry beforehand about what to say. Just say whatever is given you at the time, for it is not you speaking, but the Holy Spirit'' (Mark 13:11).

c. God's faithfulness in the past

Paul's hope was also based on previous experience. God had not failed him before, and he knew God would not fail him now. Thus he wrote, ''I eagerly expect and hope that I will . . . have sufficient courage *so that now as always* Christ will be exalted in my body'' (1:20).

Paul had escaped the jaws of death on numerous occasions. He wrote to the Corinthians that he had ''been exposed to death again and again.'' Becoming more specific, he said, "Five times I received from the Jews the forty lashes minus one. Three times I was beaten with rods, once I was stoned, three times I was shipwrecked, I spent a night and a day in the open sea, I have been constantly on the move. I have been in danger from rivers, in danger from bandits, in danger from my own countrymen, in danger from Gentiles; in danger in the city, in danger in the country, in danger at sea; and in danger from false brothers. I have labored and toiled and have often gone without sleep; I have known hunger and thirst and have often gone without food; I have been cold and naked'' (2 Cor. 11:23-27).

Through all this, Paul had never once been forsaken by the Lord. God's strength and power had accompanied Paul to endure and to be delivered. And now in a Roman prison, he was convinced that God would not forsake him.

2. *His hope explained*

Paul uses several key words and phrases in this passage to explain in more detail what his *hope* really was.

a. "Deliverance"

By *deliverance* the apostle was not talking exclusively about his freedom from prison. This is obvious from the next verse, which projects the possibility of death. But what he meant by deliverance is also clarified in this verse.

b. "In no way be ashamed"

Deliverance to Paul meant taking a stand for Jesus Christ. "I am not ashamed of the gospel," he had written to the Roman Christians on a previous occasion (Rom. 1:16). Now that he was in Rome ready to face his trial, these words were doubtless ringing in his ears. In fact, his critics — who had probably read or at least heard about his Roman letter — may have gambled that he would fail to be bold and courageous in the face of the possibility of death.

As Paul anticipated standing before the Roman magistrates, he was *confident* he would be able to practice what he had preached. In no way did he want to be intimidated and be afraid to speak clearly the message of the gospel. He wrote, "I eagerly expect and hope that I in no way will be ashamed . . ." (1:20).

c. "But will have sufficient courage"

The opposite behavior from *being ashamed* is to *have sufficient courage*. Paul contrasts his previous statement with this one. The word *courage* literally means to be "forthright in public speaking."

Again Paul probably thought of his words to the Roman Christians when he said, "I am obligated both to Greeks and non-Greeks, both to the wise and the foolish. That is why I am eager to preach the gospel also to you who are at Rome" (Rom. 1:14, 15).

Paul, of course, had been demonstrating this courage the whole time he had been chained to a guard in Rome. But the real test still lay ahead. No matter what the verdict — life or death — Paul was ready to speak for his Lord.

d. "Christ will be exalted in my body"

To think about being put to death for any reason is a difficult thought for most if not all human beings. Paul was no exception. But whether he was allowed to live, or whether he was put to death, he had one goal: "That now as always Christ will be exalted in my body."

As noted earlier, Paul had a "good track record." This was not the first time he had faced death, and he had done so courageously and for God's glory. As he considered this as a possible "final lap," he was confident he would win the race. With the prayers of the Philippians upholding him and with the Spirit of Christ directing him, he knew he would not fail his Lord in the "home stretch."[2]

B. Paul's Struggle (1:21-23)

Though Paul faced what appeared to be inevitable tragedy with eagerness, expectation, and hope, he was not without ambivalent feelings. He had an inner struggle. He put it succinctly: "For to me, to live is Christ and to die is gain" (1:21).

1. *"To live is Christ"*

Ever since Paul's conversion to Christianity, Jesus Christ had been at the center of his life. Everything Paul said and did revolved around this One he had previously hated and rejected. While many — even Christians — continued to live for self and their personal goals, Paul focused everything in Christ. For him to go on living, to escape the executioner's sword, would simply mean an opportunity to continue preaching Jesus Christ and sharing his life with others.

High on his priority list were the Philippian Christians. His hope was that he might once again visit them and minister to their needs. He wrote, "If I am to go on living in the body, this will mean fruitful labor for me. . . . It is more necessary for you [Philippians] that I remain in the body" (1:22, 24).

2. *"To die is gain"*

But herein lies Paul's struggle! Humanly speaking, and in his inner being, he does not know which to choose. "I am torn between the two," he wrote. On the one hand he knew that to remain alive would give him opportunity to continue preaching Christ and to help Christians mature in their faith, hope, and love. But on the other hand he had an intense "desire to depart and be with Christ, which," he said, "is better by far" (1:23).

Think of it! Heaven was such a reality to Paul that he could not wait to see Christ face to face — to be in His presence and enjoy the glories of heaven forever.

Obviously Paul was eager to be delivered from his imprisonment, to be set free to move about as before, carrying out the Great Commission. But more than that, Paul was eager to be "set free" from his earthly body and to be a free spirit, enjoying the glorious presence of Christ, waiting for that day when he would receive a new and glorious body — at the day of Jesus Christ, when all those who have died in Christ will be reunited with their new and glorious bodies (1 Cor. 15:50-57).

C. Paul's Decision (1:24-26)

Paul's inner struggle was soon resolved. He made his decision. He was willing to remain in the body, though personally this would be his second choice. Once again Paul's unselfish and Christ-centered attitude and philosophy of life won out. Consequently he wrote, "Convinced of this [that is, of the necessity of remaining in the body for the sake of the Philippian Christians], I know that I will remain, and I will continue with all of you for your progress and joy in the faith, so that through my being with you again your joy in Christ Jesus will overflow on account of me" (1:25, 26).

What does Paul mean? Did the Holy Spirit suddenly give him insight into his immediate future? Or did he at this moment form a judgment that he would be released from prison?

Some believe both ideas are possible interpretations. Others, however, believe he made an inner decision — a decision to be willing to remain in his body, to be willing to give up his own desire to go to heaven, and to go on living in the body so as to be able to continue his ministry to others.

All these interpretations are feasible. Paul *was* in fact released from prison. And it is possible that he *did* return to Philippi (I Tim. 1:3).

Personally I favor the last interpretation. It seems this was the resolution to Paul's struggle — a willingness to remain in the body. Previously he "was torn between the two" (1:23). He had an intense "desire to depart and be with Christ," but because of the human need he saw all around him, he became convinced it would be better to live than to die. This he was willing to do!

A TWENTIETH-CENTURY APPLICATION

This passage has many points of application. For example, we have the same sources of hope as Paul: our prayers for each other and the presence of the Holy Spirit in our lives. Though the Holy Spirit does not speak in revelation to us today as He did to Paul, He still speaks *directly* to us through the eternal Word of God. Thus every Christian can know the mind of God as he reads the Bible and applies the scriptural truth to his life.

But perhaps most significantly, this passage sets forth with unusual clarity Paul's philosophy of life. Even in the midst of a decision to go to heaven or to remain on earth he chose the latter — not just to escape pain of execution, but to serve Jesus Christ and others.

Christ was first in Paul's life. And because Christ gave His life for others, Paul too had as his primary goal to live an unselfish life. Paul said, "For to me, to live is Christ." What can you say? There are several possibilities.

A PERSONAL LIFE RESPONSE

Following is the multiple-choice statement you began this chapter with. If you were totally honest, now that you have studied Paul's philosophy of life, what word or words would *you* put in the blank? Would it be *Christ?*

FOR TO ME, TO LIVE IS_____!

a. Money   e. My house   i. Sex

b. Entertainment f. My family   j. My work

c. Friends   g. Myself   k. Sports

d. School   h. Fun   l. Other _____

Select the aspect or aspects of your life that you believe are not in proper relationship to Christ. Ask God to help you refocus your life. Pray that you will be able to carry out Christ's instructions when He said, "But seek first his kingdom and his righteousness, and all these things will be given to you as well" (Matt. 6:33).

INDIVIDUAL OR GROUP PROJECT

Review this chapter. Discuss how you as a group can make

Christ more central. For example, as a family, how can you use what God has given you to minister to others?

NOTES

[1] That Paul expected that Christ could come in his own lifetime, or within the lifetime of his friends, is clear from various New Testament passages. Philippians 1:6 is no exception.

[2] Later Paul wrote to Timothy — probably after his second imprisonment — and verified his victory: "For I am already being poured out as a drink offering, and the time has come for my departure. I have fought the good fight, I have finished the race, I have kept the faith. Now there is in store for me the crown of righteousness, which the Lord, the righteous Judge, will award to me on that day — and not only to me, but also to all who have longed for his appearing" (2 Tim. 4:6-8).

Chapter VI

United We Win, Divided We Lose

SOMETHING TO THINK ABOUT

Ask any football coach what it takes to win. If he really understands the game, he will zero in on three factors — a good defense, a good offense, and a positive attitude. Would you believe that Paul believed the same ingredients are necessary for Christians to be victorious over *their* opponents!

A LOOK AT PAUL'S LETTER . . .

A General Exhortation

1:27 Whatever happens,
conduct yourselves in a manner worthy of the
gospel of Christ

A Specific Strategy

Then, whether I come and see you
or only hear about you in my absence,
I will know that you
stand firm in one spirit ①
contending as one man for the faith of the gospel ②
1:28 without being frightened in any way ③
by those who oppose you.

Reassurance in the Battle

This is a sign to them that they will be destroyed,
but that you will be saved— ①
and that by God.
1:29 For it has been granted to you on behalf of Christ
Not only to believe on him, ②
but also to suffer for him,
since you are going through
the same struggle
you saw I had,
and
now hear that I still have.

WHAT DID PAUL SAY?

A. A General Exhortation
   —by Paul the Magistrate
   (Heavenly Citizenship)

B. A Specific Strategy
   —by Paul the Coach
   (An Athletic Contest)

   1. "Stand firm in one spirit"
      —defensive stance
   2. "Contending as one man"
      —offensive stance
   3. "Without being frightened"
      —a victorious attitude

C. Reassurance in the Battle
   —by Paul the General
   (A Life and Death Struggle)

   1. Victory is assured

   2. Double assurance

WHAT DID PAUL MEAN?

We have seen that Paul was uncertain of his immediate earthly destiny. If he had made a selfish choice, he would have gone home to heaven! But because he believed it would be more helpful for the Philippian Christians if he stayed on earth, he made that choice. He was willing to "remain in the body." And once he had settled that issue, he moved quickly to his primary concern — the spiritual welfare of the Christians at Philippi.

A. A General Exhortation — by Paul the Magistrate
(1:27) (Heavenly Citizenship)

Leaving the introductory and autobiographical section of his letter, Paul moved into a very practical section in which he gave a number of exhortations. As he often did (see Eph. 4:1; Rom. 12:1, 2), he began with a general and overarching exhortation that set the stage for more specific exhortations.[1] He wrote, "Whatever happens [to me], conduct yourselves in a manner worthy of the gospel of Christ" (1:27).

The words "conduct yourselves" alluded to the Christians' earthly associations in Philippi. The Greek word used by Paul *(politeuesthe)* often referred to job duties that a man is responsible for as a member of a community or body of people. From this word we get such English words as *politic* or *political*. Literally translated, Paul said, "Behave as citizens," or "Perform your duties as good citizens."

Paul was drawing a meaningful comparison between (1) the city of Philippi as a part of the Roman Empire and (2) the body of Christians in Philippi as a part of the kingdom of God. They would have known instinctively what he meant. The people of Philippi were proud of their privileges and rights as Roman citizens. Luke recognized their status when he identified Philippi as a "Roman colony" and a "leading city" (Acts 16:12). Later Luke recorded that the uproar which resulted in the imprisonment of Paul and Silas arose because the magistrates in Philippi thought these men were violating Roman customs (Acts 16:21).

Paul was appealing, then, to a familiar cultural and emotional mentality. "You are loyal to your city and to your country," he implied. "Then, more so, be loyal to your fellow Christians and to the eternal kingdom of God. Be a good citizen of heaven, even though you're still on earth."

How could they do this? Paul completed the exhortation in the very same breath: they are to conduct themselves in a "manner worthy of the gospel."

These are not unfamiliar words from Paul's pen — nor from his lips. Very likely he reminded Christians of their responsibility again and again as he traveled from city to city and church to church in the New Testament world (Eph. 4:1; Col. 1:10; 1 Thess. 2:12).

Just as all loyal Philippians desired to live up to their high calling and the privilege of being citizens of Rome, so the Christians in Philippi were to live up to their high calling as citizens of the kingdom of God. Thus Paul exhorted them to live "in a manner worthy of the gospel of Christ."

B. A Specific Strategy — by Paul the Coach (1:27, 28)
(An Athletic Contest)

After his general exhortation, Paul gave specific exhortations that applied directly to the problems facing the Philippian Christians. Just as quickly, he shifted metaphors. Turning from an allusion to citizenship, he drew upon the Philippians' acquaintance with athletic contests.

1. *"Stand firm in one spirit"* – *defensive stance*

Any team of athletes who compete must have a definite strategy. The opponents who are advancing must be stopped; they must not score.

Permit me to use a local illustration: Where would the Dallas Cowboys be in their lifetime pro football record without a Bob Lilly and Company? These are men who have held the line — together. But it has taken more than the "Front Four." The Cowboy defensive squad, as a whole, has not developed the reputation of "doomsday" by sitting on the bench or resting on their laurels when the ball is snapped, or by each man's doing his "own thing." No team earns a recognized title in the world of sports without performance to back it up — unified performance.

Paul encouraged the Christians at Philippi to "stand firm in one spirit" against their opponents — the opponents of the gospel of Christ. It would take more than a Christian here or there to "hold the line." It would take the *whole* "Christian team" at Philippi. *Together* they had to take a defensive stance.

And it was to be "in one spirit" — that emotional feeling that draws a team (a body of believers) together.

Many a game has been lost in the world of sports because of fractured morale. One bad attitude can destroy unity and oneness. That is why even a very skilled player can be benched and see little action. Skill is necessary, yes, but a bad attitude will undermine the "oneness of spirit" that is vital to winning.

2. *"Contending as one man" – offensive stance*

Interestingly the word *contend* actually comes from a Greek word used of an athletic contest *(sunathlountes)*. From it we get our English words *athlete* and *athletics*.

The Philippians got Paul's message fast. To win against opponents of Christianity in Philippi they not only had to take a strong defensive stance — stand firm — but also had to exert offensive effort — contend for the faith.

No athletic team can win consistently without both an offensive and defensive strategy. Again, I use an example from my hometown. Frequently Tom Landry — a Christian who is coach of the Dallas Cowboys — has emphasized the importance of both good defensive and offensive performance. On occasions when the outcome of the game has been less than happy for the Cowboys, it has often been caused by the inability of both squads to perform equally well. The "oneness" of the *whole team* has been missing.

It takes more than a good quarterback — as important as

he is. If the offensive linemen don't hold the charging defensive linemen, the quarterback is "dead." And if the running backs don't get through, the ball will not advance. And if the wide receivers don't get into the open, those gallant moments of significant forward movement fade into mere wishes and dreams. A touchdown may never come.

Paul speaks in this passage of "contending as *one man.*" No *one* Christian can win by himself; he needs other members of the body of Christ. Together as one body they must move toward victory in Jesus Christ.

Too often a local body of believers depends on "the pastor" to contend for the faith. Or they depend on the elders or some other small group in the church. Paul made it clear to the Philippians that *every* believer in Philippi was to be involved in advancing the cause of Christ.

3. *"Without being frightened"* – *a victorious attitude*
An athletic team that moves onto a playing field must do so with a positive attitude — an attitude of victory. Like it or not, a confident but realistic "we are going to win" attitude chalks up victories.

This is true in individual competition as well. You may have emotionally rebelled against what appeared to be a "bragging" Mark Spitz — but he won seven gold medals in the 1972 Olympics. You may have been even a little sickened by the egotistical antics of Muhammad Ali — but he became a world champion. And as a team — united as *one* confident mass of humanity — a Super Bowl team emerges each year, demonstrating the importance of unified effort.

Paul was a good "coach." He knew that a successful strategy against Satan's forces included more than skill and determination. It involved an attitude of confidence and trust, not in their own human efforts, but in the Lord Jesus Christ. Near the end of this epistle, he bore gallant testimony to this fact when he wrote, "I can do everything through him who gives me strength" (4:13).

Paul then exhorted the Philippians not to be afraid of their opponents. Don't be "frightened in any way," he charged.

You will win, no matter what the outcome: this Paul was sure of. Had he not just explained this truth from his own life when he spoke of his own "deliverance"? "I eagerly expect and hope," he said, "that I will in no way be ashamed, but will have sufficient courage so that now as always Christ will be exalted in my body, whether by life or by death" (1:20). Paul's constant desire for the Philippian Christians was that they, too, would have the same boldness and courage to exalt Christ in *their* bodies — no matter what the cost.

C. Reassurance in the Battle — by Paul the General (1:28-30) (A Life and Death Struggle)

1. *Victory is assured*

Metaphorically, Paul moved from political loyalty to athletic loyalty and then to the heart of the "battleground." As a faithful and steady general, he reassured the Philippian soldiers of ultimate victory in Jesus Christ. "This [that is, their defensive and offensive stance, coupled with an attitude void of fear] is a sign to them [their opponents] that they will be destroyed, but that you will be saved — and that by God."

Paul well knew the Roman mind. Loyalty, determination, and boldness were marks of their civic pride and dedication to their national emperor and local magistrates. Inherent in the Philippian Christians' willingness to choose between loyalty to an earthly kingdom and a heavenly kingdom was a powerful message of truth. The message would be loud and clear to the persecutors in Philippi; the sign was one of victory. They couldn't miss the reality of these Christians' commitment and willingness to die for Jesus Christ. They could not miss the *unified* determination to stand for Jesus Christ no matter what the cost. This truly was the "final apologetic."

When Paul used the word *sign*, some believe he was actually alluding to the "thumbs up" or "thumbs down" signal, when the fickle crowd in the Roman amphitheater signified their desire for a gladiator to "live" or "die." If so, Paul was saying to the Philippians that God would be giving the signal — through them, as they "stand firm in one spirit, contending as one man for the faith of the gospel without being frightened in any way'' — that their opponents' doom was sealed. The foe would ultimately be destroyed if they did not repent and turn to Jesus Christ in faith. Furthermore, Paul said that the Christians' future was also predetermined: they would ''be saved — and that by God.''

2. Double assurance

Christians need not experience persecution at the hands of the opponents of Christianity to be assured of the reality of their faith. But when they do, Paul implied, it is ''double assurance'' and a privilege. Hence Paul wrote, ''For it has been *granted* to you on behalf of Christ *not only to believe* on him, *but also to suffer for him.* . . .''

Belief is enough to be assured of heaven. ''Since we have been justified through faith, we have peace with God through our Lord Jesus Christ,'' Paul wrote to the Romans (5:1). But, he said, when you *suffer too,* be doubly assured you are in God's family.

Paul reminded the Philippians of his own persecution when he was first with them — his imprisonment and beatings at the hands of the magistrates (Acts 16:22-30). Remember, he said, the ''same struggle you saw I had'' (1:30).

Cannot you hear the ''former'' Philippian jailer as he heard this letter read? ''I remember!'' he thought with a reassuring tone of reminiscence. ''I can testify and verify that my faith in Christ was prompted, not just by the earthquake, but by the boldness for Christ and the loyalty and integrity of Paul and Silas. It was their steadfast faith in Christ, even as Roman citizens, in the midst of persecution that helped convince me of the reality of Christianity.''

Paul concluded this paragraph by reminding the Philippians in this letter that he was still having the same struggle — right then as he wrote — in a Roman prison. Furthermore, he had just reminded them in preceding paragraphs that what had happened to him in Rome had ''really served to advance the gospel'' (1:12).

A TWENTIETH-CENTURY APPLICATION

Though many Christians over the years have been persecuted — just as the Philippians were — the majority have not been called upon by God to suffer in this way. No doubt He has reserved for a chosen few that *privilege* — a word that is difficult to write in the context of freedom as we know it in America.

Humanly speaking, no one desires to suffer. In fact, it is God's will that we pray "for kings and all those in authority, that we may live peaceful and quiet lives in all godliness and holiness. This is good," wrote Paul to Timothy, "and pleases God our Savior, who wants all men to be saved and to come to a knowledge of the truth" (1 Tim. 2:1-3).

Very likely more people are won to Christ by unity in the midst of *peace,* than by unity in the midst of *persecution.* But as we have seen, both bring results.

More applicable to the average situation today, perhaps, is our attitude as Christians toward the "minor persecutions" that come our way. How easy it is to shrink back from even casual rejection by the non-Christian world. Or, how many Christians there are who are easily hurt by feeling they are neglected, even by other Christians. How self-centered and supersensitive we have become!

A PERSONAL LIFE RESPONSE

What can you do as a Christian to apply the truth of this passage of Scripture — right now in your workaday world and in your church? Consider making this covenant with God:

"First, by God's grace, I will do all I can to conduct myself as a member of my own local body of believers in a manner worthy of the gospel of Christ. More specifically, I will do all I can to help my local church *stand firm in one spirit* and to *contend as one man* for the faith of the gospel, and to do all I can to overcome the *insecurity and fear* that may cause me to draw back from doing *whatever* God wants me to do to advance the gospel of Christ."

Signed: _____

INDIVIDUAL OR GROUP PROJECT

What specific steps must be taken? Read Philippians 2:1-11. Notice in this passage how an attitude of unity and oneness can actually be developed within a body of Christians.

NOTES

[1] By way of comparison, Paul began this letter to the Philippians with autobiographical material and then moved quickly into the practical section of his letter. But, when he wrote to the Ephesians and Romans, he majored on doctrinal teaching and then moved into practical exhortations. This, it seems again, helps demonstrate the maturity level of the church at Philippi. They were no doubt well grounded in spiritual truth.

Chapter VII
Unity in Christ

SOMETHING TO THINK ABOUT

Have you ever stopped to ask yourself what Satan's most significant strategy has been since early New Testament days? Where has he concentrated his efforts in order to thwart the work of Christ the most? What has he done? And why?

The next paragraphs in Paul's letter to the Philippians helps make the answers to these questions quite clear.

A LOOK AT PAUL'S LETTER . . .

The Basis for Christian Unity

2:1 If you have any encouragement from being united with
Christ,

if any comfort from his love,
if any fellowship with the Spirit,
if any tenderness and compassion,

The Steps to Christian Unity

2:2 then make my joy complete by being like-minded,
having the same love,
being one in spirit and purpose.

2:3 Do NOTHING out of selfish ambition or vain conceit,
but in humility consider others better than yourselves.

2:4 Each of you should look not only to your own interests,
but also to the interests of others.

An Example to Follow

2:5 Your attitude should be the same as that of Christ Jesus:

2:6 Who, being in very nature God,
did not consider equality with God something
to be grasped, ①

2:7 but made himself nothing,
taking the very nature of a servant, ②
being made in human likeness.

2:8 And being found in appearance as a man,
he humbled himself
and became obedient to death —③
even death on a cross!

2:9 Therefore God exalted him to the highest place ④
and gave him the name that is above
every name,

2:10 that at the name of Jesus every knee should bow,
in heaven and on earth and under
the earth, and every tongue confess
that Jesus Christ is Lord,
to the glory of God the Father.

WHAT DID PAUL SAY?

A. The Basis for Christian Unity — Our Personal Benefits in Christ
  1. Encouragement from being united with Christ
  2. Comfort from Christ's love
  3. Fellowship with the Spirit
  4. Tenderness and compassion

B. The Steps to Christian Unity
  1. Be like-minded
  2. Have the same love
  3. Be one in spirit and purpose

  4. Be unselfish and humble

C. An Example to Follow — Jesus Christ

  1. His unselfish behavior

  2. His unprecedented humility

  3. His sacrificial attitude

  4. His glorious exaltation

WHAT DID PAUL MEAN?

In the previous paragraph, Paul exhorted the Philippian Christians to "stand firm in one spirit" and to contend "as one man for the faith of the gospel" — in short, to be *one* in Christ and to maintain *unity* amid persecution. But some of the Christians in Philippi — if they were human at all — may have been tempted to ask *why*. Others may have asked *how* this could be done.

Paul anticipated these questions. First he laid down some basic *reasons* for unity, and then he gave them *concrete steps* — specific exhortations regarding *how* to create this unity.

A. The Basis of Christian Unity — Our Personal Benefits in Christ (2:1)

Paul did something in the Philippian letter he had done on other occasions: he built a case for his exhortation. For example, in writing to the Roman Christians he urged them to live a *sacrificial life* for Christ on the basis of Christ's *sacrificial love* for them. "In view of God's mercy," Paul wrote, "I urge you . . . to offer yourselves as living sacrifices, holy and pleasing to God — which is your spiritual worship" (Rom. 12:1).

In a sense Paul approached the subject of commitment and dedication in the same way with the Philippians. *Why* should we "stand firm in one spirit" and contend "as one man"? Paul anticipated this question, and gave the Philippians four basic reasons.

1. *Encouragement from being united with Christ*

Paul seems to use an indirect grammatical technique in laying down his argument for unity. "*If* you have any encouragement . . . *if* any comfort . . . *if* any fellowship . . . *if* any tenderness and compassion, *then* . . ."

To get hold of what Paul said, suppose you have attended a Christian college that has meant a great deal to you. In fact, you came to know Christ there. The Christian professors helped you learn to live for Christ in a mature way. You met a wonderful girl there who became your wife — or you met a tremendous man who became your husband. And you were given the necessary training to prepare you for a life vocation.

Now you are graduating! As you do, I approach you and say, *"If* you have been encouraged at all in this school, *if* you appreciate what you've learned, *if* you are grateful for the environment that enabled you to meet a fine Christian person to become your mate, *if* you are grateful for the preparation for a life vocation, *then* be sure to support this school with your prayers and financial resources."

If these circumstances were true, few there are who would not get the message I was trying to communicate about their responsibility to their alma mater. In the same way, the Philippian Christians had no problem *hearing* what Paul was saying!

Paul's first appeal, then, was to the encouragement these Philippian Christians had received "from being united with Christ." They were no longer without hope in the world. "You will be saved!" Paul had just stated (1:28).

Think of Lydia: she was so excited about her new faith that she encouraged Paul, Silas, and Timothy to use her home as a base for their missionary operations in Philippi. Think of the little slave girl who was set free from the chains of an evil spirit. And think of the jailer who was converted along with his whole household: Luke records that after this remarkable experience with Jesus Christ, this man brought Paul and his fellow missionaries into his home, "set a meal before them, and the whole family *was filled with joy, because they had come to believe in God"* (Acts 16:34).

Paul therefore reminded the Philippians of the *encouragement* they had experienced "from being united with Christ."

2. *Comfort from Christ's love*

To be "united with Christ" through conversion is just one

of the benefits of being a Christian. Once we are a part of the family of God, we become beneficiaries of Christ's *continual* love and care.

True, the Philippian Christians had experienced suffering and persecution. But they had also experienced the comfort that comes from Christ's unconditional love. Perhaps Epaphroditus had shared with Paul the ways in which Christ had preserved them and helped them during this period of persecution.

3. *Fellowship with the Spirit*

The Philippians knew what it meant to experience relational Christianity, both at the divine and human levels. They were united not only to Christ, but to each other. "For we were all baptized by one Spirit into one body," Paul wrote on another occasion (1 Cor. 12:13).

This is one of the most important benefits of being a Christian. The apostle John wrote, "We proclaim to you what we have seen and heard, so that you also may have fellowship with us. And our fellowship is with the Father and with his Son, Jesus Christ" (1 John 1:3).

4. *Tenderness and compassion*

The whole Christian message is one of *tenderness* and *compassion*. Christ's unprecedented and incomparable love is at the heart of the Incarnation. "For God so loved the world that he gave his one and only Son" (John 3:16).

Yet a proper view of the Christian experience — our conversion, Christ's unconditional love and care for us as His children, and our position as a member of the body of Christ — also *produces* tenderness and compassion in the hearts of believers.

This appears to be Paul's appeal to the Philippians. He already knew they were a *caring* church: they had demonstrated this from the beginning. So he gently reminded them of what they had already experienced — using this as a basis for the exhortations to follow.

B. The Steps to Christian Unity — Do for Others What Christ Has Done for You (2:2-4)

To this point Paul's appeal to the Philippians could be paraphrased as follows: "If you have experienced encouragement from being Christians (and I know you have), if you have experienced comfort from Christ's continual and unconditional love and care (and I know you have), and if you have enjoyed your relationships within Christ's body (and I know you have), and if Christ's tenderness and compassion toward you has created any tenderness and compassion toward others (and I truly know it has), then do for others what Christ has done for you."

After establishing a basis for Christian unity by laying down several basic doctrinal propositions, Paul then applied these truths to the daily lives of the Philippian Christians. This was a common Pauline strategy. With the *doctrinal* he always gave the *practical*. Christians must not only *know*, but *do!*

But before he gave them basic steps to Christian unity, he subtly slipped in one more reason why they should walk in it. It was a personal reason — his own happiness. "Then make my joy complete . . ." (2:2).

Thus far in this letter Paul had mentioned his own personal happiness and joy *three* times, for various reasons. First, "I always pray with *joy* because of your *partnership in the gospel* from the first day until now" (1:4). Second, "The important thing is that in every way, . . . *Christ is preached*. And because of this I *rejoice*" (1:18). Third, "I will continue to *rejoice,* for I know that through your prayers and the help given by the Spirit of Jesus Christ, what has happened to me will turn out for *my deliverance*" (1:18,19). Now he adds a fourth factor that would make his joy complete — a continued *unity and oneness* in the local body of Christ at Philippi.[1]

How then can this unity be created and maintained? Interestingly Paul had just written about *four benefits* the Philippians had because of their relationship to Christ. He then gave four basic steps to guarantee unity in the body. Though it is difficult to see *exact* correlations between each of these points, the overall correlation is obvious, as indicated in the following chart:

The Basis for Christian Unity (Our personal benefits in Christ) Philippians 2:1	**The Steps to Christian Unity** (Do for others what Christ has done for you) Philippians 2:2-4
1. Encouragement from being united with Christ (our salvation and position in Christ)	1. Be like-minded
2. Comfort from His love (Christ's continual and unconditional love and care)	2. Have the same love
3. Fellowship with the Spirit (relational experiences as members of Christ's body)	3. Be one in spirit and purpose
4. Tenderness and compassion (love and concern for one another in the body)	4. Be unselfish and humble

1. *Be like-minded*

To be "like-minded" means to "think alike" — a basic step toward creating unity. Christians, of all people, have the basis for oneness in thought and action.

Christ spoke of this concept dramatically in His prayer to the Father shortly before His death. "I have given them [the disciples] your word . . . ," He prayed. "Sanctify them by the truth; your *word* is truth" (John 17:14, 17). Christ laid the foundation for "like-mindedness" with the Word of God. It was a startling message, that He *was* from God — yes, that He had come to be the Savior of the world. This message was the ultimate basis for Christian unity, not only among the disciples, but among all Christians throughout the Christian era.

Note Christ's verification of this truth as He continued His prayer: "My prayer is not for them [His disciples] alone. I pray also for those [all Christians] who will believe in me through their *message,* that *all of them may be one,* Father, just as you are in me and I in you. May they also be in us so that the world may believe that you have sent me" (John 17:20, 21).

Thus, to be "united with Christ" lays the foundation for unity and "like-mindedness." Christians have a common basis, a common message around which to build their thoughts and life-style. As Christ was *one with God,* so we can be *one with one another.*

2. *Have the same love*

Because of our position in Christ, He loves us continually and unconditionally. Nothing "will be able to separate us from the love of God that is in Christ Jesus our Lord" (Rom. 8:38, 39).

Paul exhorts the Philippians to *love as Christ loves* — not conditionally, not only when others love us. Conditional love is easy, but it is difficult to love when we are rejected or criticized.

The supreme mark of Christian maturity is love. It is the greatest of all; it includes the attitudes and actions spelled out by Paul in 1 Corinthians 13, such as patience, kindness, concern, humility, gentleness, objectivity, fairness, honesty, and sincerity. In summary, "It always protects, always trusts, always hopes, always perseveres" (1 Cor. 13:7). This, said Paul, creates Christian unity — his next exhortation.

3. *Being one in spirit and purpose*

"Like-mindedness" (thinking alike) and "loving attitudes and actions" can produce only one result — a oneness in the body of Christ. This is the true *koinonia* with and in the Spirit. Christ's great prayer to the Father for His body was "that they may be one as we are one: I in them and you in me. May they be brought to complete unity to let the world know that you sent me and have loved them even as you have loved me'' (John 17:22, 23). This is the oneness in spirit and purpose Paul was asking for in the Philippian church.

4. *Be unselfish and humble in all relationships*

How does all of this actually happen — this ''being like-minded, having the same love, being one in spirit and pur-pose''? You must, answered Paul, ''do nothing out of selfish ambition or vain conceit, but in humility consider others better than yourselves. Each of you should look not only to your own interests, but also to the interests of others'' (2:3, 4). In short, said Paul, you must be *unselfish and humble in all relationships*.

These are not new thoughts from the Apostle Paul. To the Roman Christians he wrote, ''Do not think of yourself more highly than you ought, but rather think of yourself with sober judgment, in accordance with the measure of faith God has given you'' (12:3). And to the Corinthian Christians Paul wrote, ''The eye cannot say to the hand, 'I don't need you!' And the head cannot say to the feet, 'I don't need you!' . . . But God has combined the members of the body . . . so that there should be *no division in the body,* but that its parts should have equal concern for each other'' (1 Cor. 12:21, 24, 25).

This, too, was Paul's message to the Philippian Christians — a call to continual and increased oneness and unity in the body of Christ.

C. An Example to Follow (2:5-10)

Paul's next words to the Christians in Philippi comprise one of the most profound passages in the New Testament. It is often called by Bible scholars the ''Kenosis passage.'' The word *kenosis* in Greek means ''to empty.'' Paul wrote here about the way in which Christ ''emptied Himself'' when He became incarnate in humanity.

These verses in themselves could comprise the basis for a whole chapter — or better yet, a whole book. But to get involved in all the intricacies of the Incarnation could easily interfere with our being able to understand the primary reason Paul was writing about this event — that is, to illustrate for the Philippians how each of them should relate to other members of the body of Christ. Thus Paul wrote, ''Your attitude should be the same as that of Christ Jesus'' (2:5). Our Savior, Paul said, is the supreme example in demonstrating an attitude that contributes to the development of unity and oneness in the body of Christ.

What then were these qualities in Christ's behavior?

1. *His unselfish behavior*

Christ in His preincarnate state was in ''very nature God.'' He experienced an ''equality with God'' that was not characterized by human dimensions. The apostle John told us that Christ always existed and ''was with God'' and ''was God.'' Further, John tells us that ''through him all things were made'' — including man (John 1:1, 3).

This, of course, we cannot understand in our finite minds. We can only accept the fact that it is true, and recognize that *if it were not true,* Christianity would be the same as any other religion. It would simply be another philosophy of life that in most instances, if not in all, was created and promoted by a religious leader for selfish reasons. Its source would be *earth,* not *heaven.*

But not Christianity. Its source was *unselfishness* personified in ''Christ Jesus: Who, being in very nature God, did not consider equality with God something to be grasped'' (2:6). He was willing to give up this heavenly position to occupy also an earthly position — to identify with the very ones He had created.

Paul was saying to the Philippian Christians: be unselfish in your attitudes toward other members in the body of Christ just as Christ was unselfish in His willingness to identify with lost humanity through the Incarnation.

2. *His unprecedented humility*

Another attitude demonstrated by Christ was a willingness

to make "himself nothing, taking the very nature of a servant, being made in human likness" (2:7).

Does this mean Christ became less than God? Not at all! Rather, He became *both* God and man. But He left the glories of heaven to do it. He was born into this world as any other human being, with the exception that His father was God. And He chose a lowly maiden to be His human mother. He did not come as a king, born of royalty, but as a servant. His first earthly home was a stable surrounded by animals. His parents were lowly peasants, and His first visitors were lowly shepherds. Probably two whole years went by before He made contact with anyone with royal blood — the wise men from the East.

This is *humility* personified. Thus Paul wrote to the Philippians to be like Christ in their attitudes toward other members of the body of Christ. Be humble: this will create oneness and unity.

3. *His sacrificial attitude*

To give up the glories of heaven: this is *unselfishness*. To be born as man: this is *humility*. But to die on a cross for the sins of the world: this is the greatest sacrifice known anywhere in the universe. To imitate this attitude is the most significant ingredient for creating unity among Christians.

This is why Paul considered it a privilege to suffer for Christ. This is why he said of Epaphroditus, "Welcome him in the Lord with great joy, and honor men like him, because he almost died for the work of Christ, risking his own life to make up for the help you could not give me" (Phil.2:29,30). This is also why Paul wrote, "I want to know Christ and the power of his resurrection and the fellowship of sharing in his sufferings, becoming like him in his death" (3:10). This was not some psychological "death-wish," a carry-over from his guilt for persecuting Christians. Rather, it was a true demonstration of love, a sacrificial attitude toward others in the body of Christ and toward Christ himself. Paul wrote, "But even if I am being poured out like a drink offering on the sacrifice and service coming from your faith, I am glad and rejoice with all of you." He continued, "So you too should be glad and rejoice with me" (Phil. 2:17, 18).

4. *His glorious exaltation*

Once Paul began the story of Christ's incarnation to illustrate proper attitudes in the body of Christ, he could not refrain from discussing Christ's exaltation and glorification. God honors *unselfishness, humility,* and *sacrificial attitudes,* even within the Godhead. Consequently the Father gave the Son a "name that is above every name." And someday when that name is shouted from one end of the universe to the other, *every knee will bow* and *every tongue will confess* that "Jesus Christ is Lord, to the glory of God the Father" (2:9-11).

Note that Paul said nothing about the future exaltation of the Christian. It is only implied. This, it seems, is a reflection of the very attitude Paul was asking for and the one he was demonstrating as he wrote. Unselfishness, humility, and sacrificial attitude focus on the present, on others. To talk about future glorification and rewards for the Christian in this context would be out of place.

Don't misunderstand! God *will* honor faithful service. Even a cup of water given to someone in the name of Christ will not go unnoticed. But to serve for rewards per se is selfish; it is not unconditional love for the One who died that we might live.

Remember, too, that Christ Himself, in His self-imposed limitations, was willing to experience separation from the Father for the sake of sinful man. His future *exaltation* was not part of His motivation. Thus we can understand more fully why Paul — who wanted so much to be like Christ in every way — could write to the Roman Christians and say, "I have great sorrow and unceasing anguish in my heart. For I could wish that I myself were cursed and cut off from Christ for the sake of my brothers, those of my own race, the people of Israel" (Rom. 9:2, 3).

Can there be any doubt in any Christian's heart that an

attitude like Christ's is a secret to unity and oneness in the body of Christ?

A TWENTIETH-CENTURY APPLICATION

1. How much do I appreciate the benefits I have from being a Christian?
2. Am I so involved in my own "little world" that I tend to forget the daily blessings I receive from Christ, such as —
   a. My secure position in Christ?
   b. His unconditional and abiding love (even though I fail)?
   c. The opportunities for fellowship with God, at any time?
   d. The opportunities for fellowship with other Christians, in freedom?
   e. Christ's tenderness and compassion in dying for me on the cross?
3. Am I doing all I can to contribute to the unity of Christ's body —
   a. By attempting to think as mature Christians think?
   b. By loving as Christ loves (unconditionally) instead of just when I'm loved?
4. How do I measure up to Christ's example —
   a. In His unselfish behavior?
   b. In His humility?
   c. In His sacrificial attitude?

A PERSONAL LIFE RESPONSE

Reflect on the questions just stated. Isolate the *one* aspect of your life in which you are having the most difficulty relating to other members of the body of Christ — be it family members or members of the larger body of Christians. Then spend time praying and asking God to help you change that aspect of your life — beginning now.

INDIVIDUAL OR GROUP PROJECT

Read Philippians 2:12-18. How does this message on Christian unity from Philippians 2:1-11 relate to our Christian witness as described by Paul in Philippians 2:14-16? What relationship if any do you see between Paul's illustration of Christ in Philippians 2:5-8 and Christ's words in John 13:34 and 17:20-23?

NOTES

[1] Many commentators emphasize at this point that Paul's stress in Philippians 2:1-11 seems to indicate that there must have been a significant lack of harmony and unity in Philippi. They use Paul's exhortation to Euodia and Syntyche in 4:2 as a proof text. However, the overall tone of this epistle doesn't seem to support this conclusion. Every body of believers in its incomplete state has its elements of disagreement; this was true at Philippi. But of all the New Testament churches, Paul's references to the love and concern in Philippi seem to indicate that this church had reached an outstanding state of spiritual maturity. Paul is, therefore, in his exhortation to unity in Philippians 2:1-11, encouraging a continual and even greater oneness — especially in view of their present persecution which could cause a division in the body.

Chapter VIII

A Witness in the World

SOMETHING TO THINK ABOUT

Christian unity is the basis for an effective Christian witness (John 17:23). To destroy this unity has been Satan's strategy from the earliest days of Christianity. Unfortunately, to a great extent he has succeeded in achieving his goals.

Do not misunderstand. When Christ prayed for oneness in the body in John 17:23, He was not referring to ecumenical unity. Ecumenical unity is not really a *visible* unity, even in our present culture. But the unity Christ prayed for *was* visible. And this can be true only through dynamic local bodies of believers — like the church in Philippi.

Paul's General Exhortation Regarding Their Christian Witness

2:12 Therefore, my dear friends,
    as you have always obeyed —
                not only in my presence,
                but now much more in my absence —
        continue to work out your salvation with
        fear and trembling,   B1
2:13   for it is God who works in you to will and do what
        pleases him.   ②

Paul's Specific Exhortations Regarding Their Christian Witness

2:14 Do everything without complaining or arguing, B2
2:15 so that you may become blameless and pure, B3
    children of God without fault in a crooked and de-
    praved generation,

    in which [crooked and depraved generation] you shine
        like stars in the universe B4
2:16 as you hold out the word of life —

Paul's Reward Because of Their Christian Witness
    in order that I may boast on the day of Christ
①   that I did not run or labor for nothing.
2:17 But even if I am being poured out like a drink offering
②   on the sacrifice and service coming from your faith,
        I am glad and rejoice with all of you.
2:18 So you too should be glad and rejoice with me.

WHAT DID PAUL SAY?

A. Paul's General Exhortation Regarding Their Christian Witness

   1. Man's human responsibility

   2. God's divine enablement

B. Paul's Specific Exhortations Regarding Their Christian Witness
Work out your salvation . . .
1. With fear and trembling (see v. 12)
2. Without complaining or arguing
3. Becoming blameless and pure and without fault

4. Shining like stars in the universe

C. Paul's Reward Because of Their Christian Witness

1. In the future

2. In the present

WHAT DID PAUL MEAN?

In several paragraphs in this epistle Paul exhorted the Philippians regarding their *individual* and *corporate* Christian conduct — particularly as it related to the unbelieving world. They were to conduct themselves "in a manner worthy of the gospel of Christ" (1:27). They were to "stand firm in one spirit, contending as one man for the faith of the gospel" — and, said Paul, "without being frightened in any way by those who oppose you" (1:27, 28). In all these relationships — both within the body of Christ and with those outside the body of Christ — they were to imitate Christ's unselfish, humble, and sacrificial life — which, said Paul, will result in love and unity (2:2-8).

Paul then became more specific and practical about their relationships with non-Christians. If you read verses 12-18 casually, it may appear that Paul was continuing to talk about *relationships within the body* — as he was earlier in verses 2-4. But when you read more carefully, it becomes clear that in the verses before us he was speaking of the Philippian Christians' *relationships to the world* — their Christian witness. Note the following comparisons, especially the different words Paul used and the different environment he had in mind:

Relationships Within the Body (Philippians 2:2-4)	**Relationships With the World** (Philippians 2:12-16a)
Then make my joy complete by being *like-minded*, having *the same love*, being *one in spirit and purpose*. Do nothing out of *selfish ambition* or *vain conceit*, but in *humility consider others better than yourselves*. Each of you should look not only to your own interests, but also to the interests of others.	Continue to work out your salvation with *fear and trembling*. . . . Do everything without *complaining or arguing*, so that you may become *blameless and pure*, children of God *without fault in a crooked and depraved generation*, in which you *shine like stars* in the universe as you *hold out the word of life*.

A. Paul's General Exhortation Regarding Their Christian Witness (2:12, 13)

Paul began this paragraph with a note of encouragement and positive feedback — a marked characteristic of the writer. He calls them "dear friends" — a sign of his deep affection for them. He commended them for their obedience when he was with them and then, in a subtle but honest way, let them know that he believed they would continue to obey Christ, even more in his absence than when he was there.

Paul then spoke directly of his concern. He exhorted these Christians to be witnesses for Christ from two perspectives. First, *they were to work out their salvation* — pinpointing *human responsibility*. Second, they were to realize that *God was at work within them* — emphasizing their *divine resources*. Both are vitally important to our Christian witness.

1. Man's human responsibility

When Paul told the Philippians to "work out" their salvation, they did not interpret this as an exhortation to "work *for*" their salvation." This is impossible. On another occasion Paul wrote, "For it is by grace you have been saved, through faith — and that not from yourselves, it is the gift of God — not by works, so that no one can boast" (Eph. 2:8, 9).

Rather, Paul exhorted them to "live out" their Christianity in such a way that those who did not know Christ would either be attracted to their lives and to the truth that had made them what they were — or they would at least *know* that Christ had revealed Himself as the Savior for lost humanity and wants to live in the hearts and lives of those who respond to Him in faith. This is undoubtedly what Paul had in mind when he stated earlier in this letter, "This is a sign to them that they will be destroyed, but that you will be saved" (Phil. 1:28).

The important point is that man is responsible to share Christ with non-Christians. What is *inside* must come *outside*.

2. God's divine enablement

Christian witness, however, is not purely a human affair —

man's ingenious effort in communication. It has a divine dimension. More important than human effort is the marvelous truth that God lives in us and desires to work through us. Thus, after exhorting the Philippians to *work out* their salvation, Paul wrote, "It is *God* who works in you to will and do what pleases him" (2:13).

This also correlates with the Ephesians passage. After emphasizing that salvation is by grace and "through faith" and "not by works," Paul wrote, "For we are God's workmanship, created in Christ Jesus *to do* good works, which God prepared in advance for us to do" (Eph. 2:10).

Therefore we see a divine balance that permeates Scripture — man's human responsibility blended with God's divine resources. Here Paul was talking about keeping this balance in Christian witness. But how important to keep these two dimensions in balance no matter what our responsibilities, circumstances, and goals!

B. Paul's Specific Exhortations Regarding Their Christian Witness (2:14-16)

Paul used several words and phrases to describe the relationship the Philippians were to have with non-Christians. All are closely related in meaning, and each statement leads naturally to the next and adds to the overall attitude Paul wanted the Philippians to have toward unbelievers.

1. *"With fear and trembling"* [or respect and fear]

"Continue to work out your salvation with *fear and trembling*," Paul wrote.

Interestingly these words (fear and trembling) are the very same Greek words (*phobou* and *tromou*) Paul used to describe the attitudes the Ephesian slaves were to have toward non-Christian masters. "Slaves, obey your earthly masters with *respect and fear* [fear and trembling], and with sincerity of heart, just as you would obey Christ. Obey them not only to win their favor when their eye is on you, but like slaves of Christ, doing the will of God from your heart" (Eph. 6:5,6).[1]

Significantly, Peter used the first of these words to describe what a Christian wife's attitude toward her *unsaved* husband should be — an attitude that will help her gain a positive response from him toward the gospel of Christ. He wrote, "Wives, in the same way be submissive to your husbands so that, if any of them do not believe the word, they may be won over without talk by the behavior of their wives, when they see the purity and *reverence* [fear] of your lives" (1 Peter 3:1, 2).

What then was Paul saying when he exhorted the Philippians to work out their salvation with "fear and trembling"? The immediate context, as well as the larger context of Scripture, seems to indicate that he was speaking of having an attitude of reverence and respect toward non-Christian masters. It was not speaking of an overwhelming "fear" and "trembling" as we use these words today; rather it was the kind of attitude toward these individuals that we should have toward Christ's authority in our lives. That is why Paul exhorted the Ephesians to obey their non-Christian masters just as they "would obey Christ."

Paul made this concept even clearer in the Colossian letter when he wrote, "Slaves, obey your masters in everything; and do it, not only when their eye is on you and to win their favor, but with *sincerity of heart* and *reverence* for the Lord. Whatever you do, work at it with all your heart, *as working for the Lord,* not for men, since you know that you will receive an inheritance from the Lord as a reward. *It is the Lord Christ you are serving*" (Col. 3:22-24).

2. *"Without complaining or arguing"*

The great temptation of any Christian, especially when he is asked by a non-Christian to do something difficult, is to complain and argue. This was true of the Philippians, some of whom were apparently slaves in the Roman system. As in Colosse and Ephesus, they were "not their own." They were probably persecuted and put under great pressure, naturally resulting in a tendency to murmur and complain about their state of being.

There is another significant correlation here with the 1 Peter passage. Wives were to *respect* and *reverence* their unsaved husbands. They were to adorn themselves with "the unfading beauty of a gentle and quiet spirit, which," said Peter, "is of great worth in God's sight" (1 Peter 3:4). A "gentle and quiet spirit," of course, is the opposite of "complaining and arguing." This is the way, he said, to win them over.

Paul exhorted the Philippians, therefore, to respect and reverence these ungodly Romans and to do what they asked without negative attitudes and behavior. He then gave the reason *why!*

3. *"Become blameless and pure . . . without fault"*

"Do everything without complaining or arguing," Paul wrote, "so that you may become *blameless and pure,* children of God *without fault* in a crooked and depraved generation in which you *shine like stars in the universe* as you hold out the word of life" (2:14-16a).

To be *blameless* was a significant goal for Paul in his own life and ministry. When he wrote to the Thessalonians he reminded them that he and his fellow missionaries had lived "holy, righteous, and *blameless*" lives among these believers. It means to live in such a way that people cannot point a finger of criticism and accuse a Christian of violating principles he believes in.

To be *pure* and *without fault* are really synonyms Paul used to emphasize the importance of consistent Christian living. The important thing is that this kind of life style is to be a dynamic Christian witness to those in darkness — *crooked* and *depraved,* and without Christ and the light He gives.

4. *"Shine like stars in the universe"*

Paul used a dynamic culminating illustration to make his point. Christians who "live in the world" without "becoming part of the world" — Christians who mingle with and work for non-Christians with a reverent and respectful attitude, who do not complain and argue, and who live blameless and pure lives — will "shine like stars in the universe." In the midst of darkness the light of God will shine forth through their lives. The "word of life" will be set forth and communicated clearly.

Furthermore, a dynamic Christian life style builds bridges to the world for verbal communication of the gospel. That is why we are to be ready at any time to give an answer to those who ask the reason for the hope that is within us (1 Peter 3:15).

Remember, too, that stars shine forth, not just as individual stars, but as clusters. The various constellations blanket the universe and stand out as scintillating examples of God's creative hand. To the average observer there is far more interest in these "bodies" of stars than single stars.

This truth is vital to Paul's illustration. It also correlates with his emphasis on love and unity in the body of Christ in the previous paragraphs (specifically 1:27, 28; 2:2-4). Furthermore, it correlates with the whole tone of the New Testament, beginning with Jesus' words to His disciples and His prayer for His disciples. To His disciples He said, "All men will know that you are my disciples if you love one another" (John 13:35). To the Father He prayed, "May they be brought to complete unity to let the world know that you sent me and have loved them even as you have loved me" (John 17:23).

It is certainly not without significance that Paul's illustration of the Incarnation — the great Kenosis — comes in the middle of several paragraphs emphasizing unity within the body as well as positive Christian attitudes toward the non-Christian world. In some marvelous way, the Holy Spirit chose to use unity in the body of Christ as a means to explain the reality of the Incarnation: as we are one in Christ, so also Christ is one with the Father and became a man to provide eternal redemption for the world.

As we look up at the dark sky each night and see shining clusters of stars, all beautifully and intricately placed in the universe by God, so the non-Christian world should be able to look at local bodies of Christians and see the oneness and beauty of Christ reflecting the message "that God was reconciling the world to himself in Christ" (2 Cor. 5:19).

C. Paul's Reward Because of Their Christian Witness (2:17, 18)

A strong motivation in Paul's life was the prospect of meeting his Christian converts in heaven someday. To stand before the Father with these fellow-believers was all the reward he asked. This, implied Paul, is legitimate pride — not his human accomplishments, but in the fact that others are in heaven and that he would be able to present them to Christ in an act of worship and love.

Paul conveyed the same attitude when he wrote to the Thessalonians, "For what is our hope, our joy, or the crown in which we will glory in the presence of our Lord Jesus Christ when he comes? Is it not you? Indeed, you are our glory and joy" (1 Thess. 2:19).

But Paul's rejoicing was not going to be related to their presence only, but also to the fact that they had "worked out their salvation" in an honorable and fruitful way. They had truly shone like "stars in the universe" as they boldly and clearly "held out the word of life" — the message of truth about Jesus Christ. Consequently Paul said, I will be able legitimately to "boast on the day of Christ that I did not run or labor for nothing" (2:16). Their *obedience* was a sure sign of the reality of the Christian experience (2:12).

Paul didn't wait until he was in heaven to rejoice about his Christian friends. The gift he had received from the Philippians at the hand of Epaphroditus was like a down payment toward their future union in heaven. In the final verses of this paragraph Paul focused once again on the fact that he may lose his life for the cause of Christ. He considered this an opportunity for him to be a part of an offering and sacrifice to God.

Again Paul's heart and humility came through. The main

offering, he said, is the sacrifice and service coming from *your faith* — that is, the Philippians' gift to Paul and the report he had received from Epaphroditus that they were obedient to their heavenly calling amid persecution. Paul considered his death simply as the "drink offering" that would be "poured out" on *their* offering, as together Paul and the Philippians had the privilege of suffering for Jesus Christ — who set the supreme example and "became obedient to death — even death on a cross" (2:8).

A TWENTIETH-CENTURY APPLICATION

For most Christians today, particularly in America, working conditions differ considerably from those in the first century. Slavery has been abolished, thanks in part to the influence of Christianity. Opportunities for dialogue and communication, as well as protective laws, help guarantee equal and fair treatment in business and in culture generally. Though we are not yet what we should be — and never will be on this earth — as American Christians, generally speaking we surely have the best living and working conditions anywhere on earth and in all of history.

What does this say to every Christian? The principles and guidelines in this passage for Christian witness still apply and perhaps with greater force. The words of Jesus Christ come ringing home: "From those who have been given much shall much be required."

Questions to Think About

1. Am I doing my part to "work out my salvation" in the pagan community where I spend most of my time — at work, at school?
2. Do I realize as I should that God desires to work through me "to will and do what pleases Him"? And am I allowing Him to work through me?
3. Do I relate to my non-Christian employers, teachers, and others with reverence and respect, realizing that as I do, I am honoring Jesus Christ? Note that this is sometimes

difficult because, humanly speaking, some are not worthy of respect; but God says we should respect them nevertheless because they are in authority over us.

4. Do we relate to those same individuals without "complaining or agruing" so that we might "become blameless and pure, children of God without fault in a crooked and depraved generation, in which we shine like stars in the universe"?

A PERSONAL LIFE RESPONSE

Think about the above questions. Can you think of a specific situation — on your job or at school, for example — in which you have violated these guidelines of Christian witness? If so, determine today that in true humility you will apologize and ask forgiveness.

INDIVIDUAL OR GROUP PROJECT

Review this message with your family or friends. Discuss together how to handle difficult problems with non-Christians when they are overbearing and unfair, and yet be Christian in your attitudes and actions.

NOTES

[1] The translators of the New International Version translated these original words in different ways because indeed they can be used in different ways. When an original word presents various options, the translators must look carefully at the context to determine which is best. In Philippians 2:12, it seems that "respect and fear" would fit the context better. Likewise in 2 Corinthians 7:15.

Chapter IX

Timothy — A Man of Character

SOMETHING TO THINK ABOUT

When was the last time someone recommended you for a difficult task?

If you have had this experience recently, why did it happen? If you have not, why do you suppose it didn't happen?

Paul did not hesitate to recommend Timothy for a *very* difficult task. Let's see why this was true.

A LOOK AT PAUL'S LETTER . . .

Paul's Purpose in Sending Timothy to Philippi

2:19 I hope in the Lord Jesus
to send Timothy to you soon, that I also may be
cheered when I receive news about you. **②**
2:20 I have no one else like him, who takes a genuine
① interest in your welfare.

Paul's Presentation of Timothy's Character

2:21 For everyone looks out for his own interests, ⊢—**①**
not those of Jesus Christ.
2:22 But you know that Timothy has proved himself,
because as a son with his father **②**
he has served with me in the work of the gospel.

Paul's Plans for the Future

2:23 I hope, therefore, to send him as soon as I see how
things go with me. **①**
2:24 And I am confident in the Lord that I myself will come
soon. **②**

Paul's "Postscript" on Timothy

WHAT DID PAUL SAY?

A. Paul's Purpose in Sending Timothy to Philippi

1. To encourage the Philippians
2. To be encouraged by the Philippians

B. Paul's Presentation of Timothy's Character

1. His commitment to Christ's work
2. His reputation among other Christians

C. Paul's Plans for the Future

1. Regarding Timothy
2. Regarding himself

D. Paul's "Postscript" on Timothy
1. His social problem
2. His psychological problem
3. His physical problem

WHAT DID PAUL MEAN?

In this paragraph, Paul shifted his emphasis — but not completely. He *changed* his emphasis in that he moved from a series of exhortations to a discussion of Timothy and Epaphroditus, both of whom would soon leave Rome for Philippi. We see the *continuity* in Paul's emphasis, however, in that both Timothy and Epaphroditus were outstanding illustrations of what Paul had been exhorting the Philippians to do: to stand firm, to be unified, to be like-minded, and to be unselfish, humble, and sacrificial in their attitudes and actions.

Paul wrote about Timothy first. Before discussing his character, he stated clearly *why* he was sending Timothy to visit the Philippian Christians.

A. Paul's Purpose in Sending Timothy to Philippi (2:19, 20)

The apostle had two basic reasons why he wanted Timothy to visit this church. First, Paul wanted *to encourage* and minister to these believers. Because Timothy was a qualified man who could apparently leave on the journey "soon," Paul was eager for him to be on his way. "I hope in the Lord Jesus to send Timothy to you *soon*," Paul wrote. "I have no one else like him, who takes a genuine interest in your welfare" (2:19, 20).

Paul's great concern, then, was the Philippians' welfare. Because Timothy's concern for them was just as intense and sincere as Paul's, Paul chose him as his personal representative.

This was not an unusual decision for Paul. He had great confidence in Timothy. On several other occasions he had sent Timothy to help local churches. To the Corinthians he wrote, "Therefore I urge you to imitate me. For this reason I am sending to you Timothy, my son whom I love, who is faithful in the Lord. He will remind you of my way of life in

Christ Jesus, which agrees with what I teach everywhere in every church'' (1 Cor. 4:16, 17).

Moreover, to the Thessalonians Paul wrote, "So when we could stand it no longer, we thought it best to be left by ourselves in Athens. We sent Timothy, who is our brother and God's fellow worker in spreading the gospel of Christ, to strengthen and encourage you in your faith, so that no one would be unsettled by these trials'' (1 Thess. 3:1-3).

It is interesting, however, that in these letters to the Corinthians and Thessalonians, Paul does not qualify his intention to send Timothy with the little phrase "in the Lord Jesus" (Phil. 2:19). He is direct and certain about his plans.

But in the Philippian letter he *does* qualify his intentions, implying a degree of uncertainty regarding his own future. That is, Paul's great desire was to do the will of God; since he was not totally sure what that was, in light of his forthcoming trial, he cautiously but with great hope let the Philippians know what he intended to do for their welfare. "If all goes well," he implied, "Timothy will be on his way."

Paul had a second reason, however, for his plan to send Timothy to Philippi. He also wanted encouragement. I am sending Timothy, he said, so "that I *also may be cheered* when I receive news about you" (2:19). Paul's primary purpose was *their* encouragement! But his secondary purpose was *his own* happiness — which would be made greater by a positive report from Timothy when he returned to be at Paul's side.

Note that Paul did not expect a negative report. He anticipated a positive one — again reflecting that Paul had great confidence in the spiritually mature attitudes of the Philippian Christians (2:12).

B. Paul's Presentation of Timothy's Character (2:21, 22)

Though Paul had several things to say about Timothy, they can be summarized with two statements: first, he was outstanding in his *commitment* to the work of Jesus Christ; and second, he was outstanding in his *reputation* among other Christians.

1. *His commitment to Christ's work*

"I have no one else like him" (2:20). What a statement! Paul wrote, "Everyone looks out for his own interests, not those of Jesus Christ." Yet here was a young man who was totally committed to the work of the Lord.

Commentators disagree about what Paul actually meant by these statements. Did he literally mean there was "no one else in the world" like Timothy? Probably not. Rather, he was perhaps referring to those in Rome who *could* come, but who *would not* because of their own unwillingness to sacrifice the time and effort. He may also have been referring to the fact that of all those who had served with him in his missionary work, only Timothy had developed a deep relationship with the Philippians that was similar to Paul's.

Whatever Paul meant specifically, one thing is sure: Paul had great confidence in Timothy. The latter's commitment to Christ's work was outstanding. Paul knew Timothy would follow through on this assignment. Timothy had "proved himself" again and again — which leads to Paul's second basic comment about this faithful man.

2. *His reputation among other Christians*

Timothy's hometown was Lystra, a city Paul and Barnabas visited on their first missionary journey. Here Paul was first worshiped as a pagan god, then later stoned by the very crowd who worshiped him (Acts 14:11-19).

But probably the most memorable moment for Paul was when a young man named Timothy received Jesus Christ as his personal Savior. Trained in the Old Testament Scriptures from his childhood, Timothy immediately recognized the truths Paul and Barnabas were preaching and responded in faith (2 Tim. 3:14, 15; 1:5).

Even though Timothy apparently came from a home where his father was an unbeliever, he wasted no time in his spiritual development (Acts 16:1). In fact, when Paul later returned to Lystra, Timothy's reputation as a man of God had spread beyond his own city. Luke reports that "the brethren at Lystra *and* Iconium spoke well of him" (Acts 16:2).

The picture was clear in Paul's mind. Here was the man he had been looking for — a faithful missionary companion who would travel with him from town to town and help strengthen Christians, particularly through a pastoral and teaching ministry (Acts 16:3-5).

One of Timothy's most significant encounters with evangelism and edification in a pagan community was in Philippi. Here he demonstrated in an unusual way his faithfulness to Christ and to Paul, his beloved friend and father in the faith. Consequently Paul could write to the Philippians with confidence: "But you know that Timothy has proved himself, because as a son with his father he has served with me in the work of the gospel" (Phil. 2:22).

C. Paul's Plans for the Future (2:23, 24).

Paul ended this paragraph about Timothy by reiterating his plans — first regarding Timothy, then regarding himself. "I hope, therefore," he said, "to send him [Timothy] as soon as I see how things go with me. And" he added, "I am confident in the Lord that I myself will come soon" (2:23, 24).

Again Paul was cautious. His confidence was "in the Lord," not in man. He was uncertain of his future — a theme he developed consistently throughout this letter. He did not know for sure he would ever again see the Philippians on this earth.

But there was no doubt about his Christian attitude amid this uncertainty, for he had already written, "For I know that through your prayers and the help given by the Spirit of Jesus Christ, what has happened to me will turn out for my deliverance. I eagerly expect and hope that I will in no way be ashamed, but will have sufficient courage so that now as always Christ will be exalted in my body, whether by life or by death" (1:19-21).

D. Paul's "Postscript" on Timothy

At this point, and particularly from this passage in Philippians, it may appear that Timothy was living above human weakness — that he was a Mr. Super-Christian whom no one else could measure up to. Such was not the case. In other letters Paul addressed himself to Timothy's problems.

Timothy had several attributes that worked against him. First, he was a young man, which created a *social* problem: "Who is this kid?" some were no doubt asking. On one occasion Paul wrote to Timothy to encourage him — probably in a time of emotional weakness and insecurity: "Don't let anyone look down on you because you are young, but set an example for the believers in speech, in life, in love, in faith and in purity" (1 Tim. 4:12). In other words, Paul was exhorting Timothy to demonstrate that "youth" is a relative concept and that spiritual and psychological maturity are more significant criteria for measuring a man than chronological age. "But," implied Paul, "you'll have to prove it!" And Timothy did!

A second problem which Timothy had, clearly related to the first, was a sensitive nature. This problem was more *psychological* than social. He was easily threatened and intimidated. Consequently Paul at times had to "run interference" for this young man, such as when he wrote to the Corinthians, "If Timothy comes, see to it that he has nothing to fear while he is with you, for he is carrying on the work of the Lord, just as I am. No one, then, should refuse to accept him" (1 Cor. 16:10, 11).

Timothy evidently did not overcome this tendency completely. In Paul's final letter to him, shortly before Paul himself was martyred for Christ, he again wrote, reminding Timothy that "God did not give us a spirit of timidity, but a spirit of power, of love and of self-discipline. So do not be ashamed to testify about our Lord, or ashamed of me his prisoner" (2 Tim. 1:7, 8).

Timothy had still a third handicap — a *physical* weakness. He had stomach problems. Who knows? Maybe he had an ulcer! Sensitive people often do. Thus Paul said, "Stop drinking only water, and use a little wine because of your stomach and your frequent illnesses" (1 Tim. 5:23). Of course, we don't know for certain what this problem was; whatever it was, it was probably related to Timothy's sensitive nature.

So Timothy *was* a Super-Christian, yes — but he was not without problems. Despite his youth, his sensitive temperament, and his physical illness, he was totally committed to the work of Jesus Christ. Though he had many uphill battles, he did not allow his human weaknesses to stand in the way of his spiritual development and ministry.

A TWENTIETH-CENTURY APPLICATION

Following are some key questions to help make these biblical truths about Timothy personal in your own life right now. As you study these questions, you will note that Timothy would probably pass the test with flying colors. How about you?

1. What do people say about *me?* Do I get positive feedback from those *closest* to me that would indicate that I have a good reputation as a Christian — from my wife, my children, my friends? Note that feedback from those who do not know you as well is not a good test. Their feedback and judgments can be superficial. They may be impressed with your physical appearance or your "public" personality, which may not represent what you *really* are as a person.
2. Do more and more people seek me out as a person and share their lives with me? Do people trust me with confidential information?
3. Do my relationships with people grow deeper and more significant the longer they know me and the closer they get to me? Or do my relationships grow strained and shallow as people learn to know what I am really like?
4. Does my circle of close friends grow continually wider

and larger? Is there an increasing number of people who admire and trust me?

5. Do people recommend me for significant and difficult tasks without fear of my letting them down?

6. Am I using my age or some psychological or physical problem as an excuse to keep me from becoming a mature Christian personality?

A PERSONAL LIFE RESPONSE

Has this chapter helped to pinpoint a weakness in your life? If so, set up a personal goal, one that focuses on that weakness. What specific *action step* can you take this week to help you overcome this problem?

This week I am going to _____

_____.

INDIVIDUAL OR GROUP PROJECT

Review this message with several friends or your family and then discuss in more detail the questions under the "Twentieth-Century Application." In what *specific ways* can a person detect positive answers to these questions? For example, what *kind* of positive feedback reflects that a person has a good reputation? Or, what evidences point to the fact that people trust others?

Chapter X

Epaphroditus — A Man of Sacrifice

SOMETHING TO THINK ABOUT

Can you think of any time in your life when you have given — of yourself, of your money, of your time — until it hurt?

Do not misunderstand. I'm not talking about making yourself feel bad. Some people, because of their selfishness, give next to nothing, and *still* feel bad.

Rather, have you ever really given sacrificially? For example, have you ever been saving some money just for yourself — for a trip, for a new car, for a new piece of furniture — and then, because of a special need in someone else's life, given your money to meet that need?

If you have never had such an experience, you perhaps do not know much about sacrificial giving. Like most American Christians, you have probably been giving out of your "plenty" rather than your "poverty."

A LOOK AT PAUL'S LETTER . . .

His Deep Christian Relationships

2:25 But I think it is necessary
to send back to you Epaphroditus,
my brother,
fellow worker and ─①
fellow soldier,
who is also your messenger, ─②
whom you sent to take care of my needs.

His Great Sense of Responsibility

2:26 For he longs for all of you
and is distressed because you heard he was ill ①
2:27 Indeed he was ill, and almost died.
But God had mercy on him, ②
and not on him only but also on me,
to spare me sorrow upon sorrow.
2:28 Therefore I am all the more eager to send him,
so that when you see him again you may be glad
and I may have less anxiety.

His Reward for Faithful Service

2:29 Welcome him in the Lord with great joy, ①,②
and honor men like him,
2:30 because he almost died for the work of Christ,
risking his life
to make up for the help you could not give me.

WHAT DID PAUL SAY?

A. His Deep Christian Relationships

   1. With Paul

   2. With the Philippians

B. His Great Sense of Responsibility

   1. To the Philippians

   2. To Paul

C. His Reward for Faithful Service
   1. From the Philippians

   2. From Paul

WHAT DID PAUL MEAN?

If the key word to describe Paul's brief personality sketch of Timothy is *character*, then the key word to describe Epaphroditus is *sacrifice*. Though each sketch has its unique focus, both are beautiful illustrations of men who had "the mind of Christ" — an emphasis of Paul in previous paragraphs. Epaphroditus — like Timothy — was an outstanding example of humility and self-sacrifice. In fact, Epaphroditus almost made the *supreme* sacrifice: "he almost *died* for the work of Christ" (2:30).

Interestingly the Philippian letter is the only place in which Epaphroditus is mentioned in the New Testament. But in one paragraph (six short verses) Paul gave us some noteworthy insights into the life and motives of this man. For one thing, Epaphroditus was a Christian who had developed some deep Christian *relationships*. Second, he took his work seriously — he had a great sense of *responsibility*. Third, he was highly recommended for his efforts by Paul, who strongly desired that Epaphroditus be adequately *rewarded* for his faithful service.

A. His Deep Christian Relationships (2:25)

1. *His relationship with Paul*

Paul spoke first of his own relationship with Epaphroditus in significant terms: a *brother*, a fellow *worker*, and a fellow *soldier*.

The word *brother* speaks of their relationship in Christ. Like all true Christians, they were both members of God's family. As Paul said when he wrote to the Galatians, "There is neither Jew nor Greek, slave nor free, male nor female, for you are all one in Christ Jesus" (Gal. 3:28). Though Paul had the distinct privilege of being a chosen apostle, he still considered himself as one member of the body of Christ related to all others by his position in Christ.

Paul also called Epaphroditus a "fellow worker." Together they had served Jesus Christ. We do not know what Epaphroditus' position was in the Philippian church. Some believe he may have been an elder. If so, Paul's relationship with Epaphroditus as a co-worker probably began in Philippi, long before Epaphroditus had come to Rome. But this relationship reached a grand culmination when Epaphroditus visited Paul in prison and served with him there in furthering the work of Jesus Christ.

Finally, Paul called Epaphroditus a "fellow soldier." Those were not easy days in the service of Christ: Christians were hated, persecution was rampant. Together Paul and Epaphroditus had "fought the good fight." Unlike some Christians in Rome, Epaphroditus was *not* afraid or ashamed to be identified with Paul's chains, even if it meant physical harm and social rejection. To quote Paul, he was one of "the brothers in the Lord" who, because of his chains, had been "encouraged to speak the word of God more courageously and fearlessly" (Phil. 1:14).

Thus Paul spoke of a very deep relationship with this man Epaphroditus. Though Paul was in chains and Epaphroditus was free, they were drawn together as *one* in Christ.

2. *His relationship with the Philippians*

Paul spoke next of Epaphroditus' relationship with the Philippians. He was their messenger — literally, their "apostle."[1] He was the one they had chosen to carry their gift to Paul in order to meet his needs.

This speaks of trust and confidence. Perhaps it would be easier to understand the significance of this trust and confidence if we somehow realize the sacrifice the Philippian Christians made to gather together a sufficient amount of money to help Paul in his need. The Philippians — along with other Macedonian believers — were not known for their wealth. Paul described their financial status as one of "extreme poverty." Yet, Paul said, "they gave as much as they were able, and even beyond their ability" (2 Cor. 8:2, 3).

So when the Philippians heard of Paul's physical needs, they once again gathered together what they could from their meager resources. When they looked for a man to make this delivery, they chose Epaphroditus — a man they could trust and a man who best depicted their concern and love for Paul.

B. His Great Sense of Responsibility (2:26-28)

Deep relationships foster a sense of responsibility. How clear this is in the life of Epaphroditus! When he arrived in Rome, he is delivered the gift to Paul, but he also found a man who needed more than a quick visit. Evidently he decided to stay by Paul's side to see what he could do to help. So keen was the sense of responsibility — both to Paul and the Philippian brothers — that he nearly died in fulfilling that duty.

For some reason, God did not allow Paul to tell us exactly what Epaphroditus did that endangered his life. Perhaps this is so that all of us might identify with Epaphroditus and learn a lesson from this man, no matter what our circumstances.

There are several clues as to what the danger might have been. First, it was probably a physical illness, for he "almost died" (2:27). Though the Greek word for "ill" could refer to either psychological or physical illness, few *die* from psychological problems — unless the stress is so great that it results in a heart attack. But then, who knows, this may have been Epaphroditus' problem!

Second, whatever caused this problem, it involved "risking his life" (2:30). This has several implications. He could have worked *so hard* that he overextended his *body and mind,* leading to some type of physical and psychological deterioration. Or, he may have been subjected to severe persecution because of his loyalty to Paul.

Whatever the cause, Epaphroditus demonstrated unusual commitment to both Paul and the Philippians. His primary motivation was "to make up for the help" the Philippians could not give Paul because of their absence (2:30). As their messenger, Epaphroditus felt a keen sense of responsibility. He couldn't let them down, nor could he allow Paul to "go it alone."

Note, too, that "commitment to other Christians" means

commitment "to Jesus Christ." The two are so intertwined as to be inseparable. Thus Paul wrote to the Philippians that Epaphroditus "almost died *for the work of Christ*." And what was this work for Christ? It was to make up for the help the *Philippians* could not give *Paul!* (2:30). Sacrificial love *for the Philippians and Paul* became significant service *for Jesus Christ!*

Epaphroditus' sense of responsibility to the Philippians, as well as the depth of his relationship to them, is also seen in Paul's telling the Philippians about Epaphroditus' illness. "For he longs for all of you and is distressed because you heard he was ill" (2:26).

There seems to be no question about the nature of the problem Paul was talking about in this verse. Epaphroditus was *homesick*. Perhaps this is another clue to the basic cause of his physical illness. Otherwise, why would Epaphroditus be so concerned when the Philippians found out he was ill? (2:26). In other words, perhaps Epaphroditus was so homesick — a horrible kind of emotional illness when it is severe — that he became susceptible to physical deterioration as well. And when the Philippians heard of his problem, he was rather apprehensive about their reaction — perhaps afraid they would criticize him for his emotional weakness.

Thus Paul took the responsibility to help keep the communication lines open between Epaphroditus and his brothers and sisters in Christ in Philippi. To do so, he explained Epaphroditus' problem (2:26, 27a), indicating his own emotional relief that God had spared him (2:27b); he also made sure the Philippians understood that it was Paul's idea to send Epaphroditus back. "I am all the more eager to send him," Paul wrote, "so that when you see him again you may be glad and I may have less anxiety" (2:28). Perhaps Paul, too, was somewhat anxious about the Philippians' reaction to Epaphroditus' illness; after all, he had stayed on in Rome to help Paul.

But Paul also clarified something else. And this we see in the final section.

C. His Reward for Faithful Service (2:29, 30)

In his final words about this man, Paul made it very clear that Epaphroditus should be given due recognition for his sacrificial service. "Welcome him in the Lord with great joy, and honor men like him" (2:29). It almost appears that Paul is afraid the Philippians might be tempted to question Epaphroditus' Christian commitment for returning to Philippi because of homesickness. Though they loved and trusted him, they, like any group of Christians in this kind of circumstance, would be concerned about Paul's attitude. So Paul made it clear: it was *his* idea for Epaphroditus to return, and he wanted him to be welcomed joyfully and with full awareness of Epaphroditus' sacrificial service for Jesus Christ.

A TWENTIETH-CENTURY APPLICATION

Epaphroditus was a man of sacrifice. So was Paul. So was Timothy. And the Philippians, along with many New Testament Christians, knew the meaning of giving "until it hurts." This is *sacrificial* giving.

I think that most of us as American Christians do not even come close to knowing what this experience means. Though many of us give 10, 20, or even 30 percent of our income to the Lord's work, we still know where the next meal is coming from. We've always been quite sure that the next paycheck will arrive on time. And even if we get a little under the pile, most of us have a good credit rating at the bank: we can borrow to tide us over. Of course, few of us ever experience real inconvenience because we have given to help the work of Christ — either financially or through human effort.

I am not sure, then, that what most of us have done can really be called New Testament sacrifice — at least as compared with the experience of Paul, Timothy, Epaphroditus, and the Philippian Christians. Few of us have given amid "severe trial" and "extreme poverty" (2 Cor. 8:2). I do know of a few Christians who have actually borrowed money to give to the Lord's work — but that is an exception.

Should we be ashamed? Not necessarily. We are a blessed people: we should rejoice and praise God. Paul said, "I know what it is to be in need, and I know what it is to have plenty. I have learned the secret of being content in any and every situation, whether well-fed or hungry, whether living in plenty or in want" (Phil. 4:12).

So let us rejoice in our "plenty."

But if there is a specific need (and there always is), and if there is an opportunity to give for the work of Jesus Christ, and if we are unwilling to do our part, then perhaps we should evaluate our Christian commitment and thankfulness to God for what we have in Christ Jesus. We may need to ask ourselves if we are really having that New Testament experience which is vital to our spiritual growth.

A PERSONAL LIFE RESPONSE

Think of a way you can "give until it hurts," even if just a little bit. How about dipping into your savings to help meet a special need? Or, you may want to do something like what some friends of mine did — gave up an overseas vacation to support a very special need in their church.

Whatever you do, it should be between you and the Lord and those intimately involved. Do not open the door for Satan to tempt you toward pride. But on the other hand, don't hold back with the fear that someone may find out. They may need your Christian example.

Remember that the size of your gift is not the most important thing. Your heart attitude and giving according to your ability is what God honors. As someone said, "Little is much when God is in it." This is what Paul was talking about in 2 Corinthians 8 and 9.

INDIVIDUAL OR GROUP PROJECT

Read 2 Corinthians 8 and 9. What significant principles of giving are illustrated in these two chapters? In what ways can Christians apply these principles today?

NOTES

[1] Paul here uses the word *apostolos*, frequently translated *apostle*. This speaks again of Paul's lofty view of this man.

Chapter XI

The True Gospel

SOMETHING TO THINK ABOUT

Have you stopped to think recently about the fact that millions of people are diligently striving to do enough good things to get to heaven?

I cannot think of one non-Christian religion or cult that is an offshoot of biblical Christianity that does not have at its heart a philosophy of works. Human effort — doing something to become worthy of heaven — is one characteristic of all of them.

But Paul preached a gospel that was just the opposite. He taught that man can do nothing to receive eternal life — except believe!

A LOOK AT PAUL'S LETTER . . .

Paul's Warning

3:1 Finally, my brothers, rejoice in the Lord!
    It is no trouble for me to write the same things to you
        again, and it is a safeguard for you.

3:2 Watch out for those dogs, those men who do evil,
    those mutilators of the flesh.   ①

3:3 For it is we who are the circumcision,
    we who worship by the Spirit of God,
    who glory in Christ Jesus,
    and who put no confidence in the flesh —   ②

Paul's Past Experience

3:4 though I myself have reasons for such confidence.
    If anyone else thinks he has reasons to put confidence in
        the flesh, I have more:

3:5 circumcised on the eighth day,
    of the people of Israel,
    of the tribe of Benjamin,   ①
    a Hebrew of Hebrews;
    in regard to the law, a Pharisee;

3:6 as for zeal, persecuting the church;
    as for legalistic righteousness, faultless.   ②

Paul's Present Experience

3:7 But whatever was to my profit I now consider loss for
    the sake of Christ.

3:8 What is more. I consider everything a loss compared to
    the surpassing greatness of knowing Christ Jesus my
  ① Lord, for whose sake I have lost all things.
    I consider them rubbish, that I may gain Christ

3:9 and be found in him,
    not having a righteousness of my own that
        comes from the law,   ②
    but that which is through faith in Christ —
    the righteousness that comes from God and is by faith.

3:10 I want to know Christ and the power of his resurrection
        and the fellowship of sharing in his sufferings,   ③
        becoming like him in his death,

3:11 and so, somehow, to attain to the resurrection from the
    dead.

WHAT DID PAUL SAY?

A. Paul's Warning

    1. Characteristics of false teachers

    2. Characteristics of true teachers

B. Paul's Past Experience

    1. His religious inheritance

    2. His religious achievements

C. Paul's Present Experience

    1. His view of the past

    2. His new source of righteousness

    3. His new life goals

WHAT DID PAUL MEAN?

Perhaps the best introduction to this passage of Scripture is another epistle that Paul wrote — the letter to the Galatians. Negatively speaking, his greatest concern in that epistle was to deal with what he called "a different gospel" — which, he said, "is really no gospel at all" (Gal. 1:6,7). On the positive side, Paul's greatest concern was to reaffirm in the minds of the Galatians what the "true gospel" really was.

What was the difference? How can the two be distinguished? How do you recognize a false gospel — a false religion as compared with the true gospel of Christ?

In a nutshell, Paul speaks to these questions in one brief section of the Philippian letter. Obviously, from the earlier paragraphs in this epistle, the Philippian Christians were not having the same problem as the Galatians. But in Paul's view, to be forewarned is to be forearmed. And so he *warned* these believers also to be on guard.

A. Paul's Warning (3:1-3)

As Paul begins this paragraph, he seems to do so with a note of finality — as if he was about to close his letter with a final positive exhortation to "rejoice in the Lord." But then the Holy Spirit (as He obviously did on other occasions when Paul was writing) seemed to guide Paul to elaborate on something he had evidently written about earlier to the Philippians. He felt led to warn them against false teachers who were preaching a "false gospel." He did so by comparing the *false* with the *true*.[1]

1. *Characteristics of false teachers*

In essence, Paul wrote that false teachers are man-centered in their philosophy of religion. He used strong language to describe them: he called them "dogs," "men who do evil," and "mutilators of the flesh."

These rather sharp descriptive terms may shock you! But they serve to reflect Paul's distress and unhappiness with men who were deliberately leading people astray. His deep and loyal love for his fellow Christians often led him to speak out pointedly against individuals who were preaching a "false gospel" — and for selfish reasons.[2]

There are several possibilities as to why he used the word *dogs*. This is what self-righteous Jews call Gentiles. Since Paul was at that moment talking about Jews, perhaps he was "turning the tables." Remember that Paul was a Jew and, with every ethnic group, "it takes one to know one."

Or, perhaps Paul was implying that men who lead people astray in religious matters are no more sensitive than selfish animals that go about devouring others. Again, perhaps he was correlating the concept of "dogs" more specifically with the phrase "mutilators of the flesh" — men who *literally* enjoyed tearing the flesh through a perversion of the rite of circumcision.[3]

Whatever Paul meant specifically, one thing is clear: he was very displeased with those who were deliberately preaching a false gospel. So strong did he feel about this that when he wrote to the Galatians, he pronounced eternal judgment upon all such, including himself as well as spirit beings: "But even if we or an angel from heaven should preach a gospel other than the one we preached to you, let him be eternally condemned" (Gal. 1:8, 9).

In summary, the false teachers could be recognized by the fact that they had a *man-centered* approach to salvation. This is a works system: what man *does* to inherit eternal life is at the heart of their message. To clarify this, Paul spelled out how to recognize those who have the true message of Christ.

2. Characteristics of true teachers

Paul was speaking of all true believers in Philippians 3:3. "It is we," he wrote, "who are the circumcision."

Why is this true? Why this language? Paul gave three reasons. First, true teachers and believers "worship by the Spirit of God," not through some human rite. Paul reminded the Romans that a *Jew* was not *a true Jew* "if he is only one outwardly." Rather, he said, "a man is a Jew if he is one inwardly; and circumcision is circumcision of the heart, by the Spirit, not by the written code'' (Rom. 2:28, 29). In other words, God did not recognize the validity of the act of circumcision even in the Old Testament unless it reflected an inward reality and sacrifice of the heart.

Second, true teachers and believers "glory in Christ Jesus," not in man's accomplishments. A false gospel teaches that man is saved by what *he does;* the true gospel teaches that man is saved only by *what God has done* through Jesus Christ. On another occasion Paul made it very clear: "For it is by grace you have been saved, through faith — and this not from yourselves, it is the gift of God — not by works, so that no one can boast" (Eph. 2:8, 9).

Third, true teachers and believers "put no confidence in the flesh." Again Paul was driving home the truth that salvation is by grace through faith. Nothing man can do will save his soul. No amount of ritual, external conformity, or human activity can make a man good enough to stand before God as a righteous person.

These, then, are the marks of "true circumcision" — circumcision of the heart. Paul wrote that true teachers and believers can be recognized because they preach this kind of gospel — the gospel that is *Christ-centered*. They do not present a human formula for salvation, but rather a divine formula — "that God was reconciling the world to himself in Christ" (2 Cor. 5:19). Man dare not and cannot take credit for his salvation. Rather, he must give all honor and glory to Jesus Christ.

And what better source for verifying all of this than Paul himself. "Do you want a real-life illustration?" Paul seemed to ask. "Then let me tell you!" That's exactly what he did in the next paragraph of his letter.

B. Paul's Past Experience (3:4-6)

As Paul approached this paragraph, he seemed to say: "If you want a good illustration of a *man-centered approach* to religion, look at me! In fact, I challenge anyone to match me — both in inheritance and achievement!"

1. *His religious inheritance*

Paul reminded the Philippians he had been "circumcised on the eighth day." Before he was able to do anything for himself, his parents had followed the letter of the law (Lev. 12:3). Furthermore, he said, I am "of the people of Israel." He was no proselyte, no convert to Judaism: he was part of the chosen race from birth.

What's more, he was "of the tribe of Benjamin" — the tribe that was highly regarded in Israel because of its unusual faithfulness to the law of God. Then, too, the first king of Israel, Saul, was a Benjamite and significantly Paul's name before he was converted to Christ was also Saul. Perhaps his parents so desired that he be a "great" in Israel that they named him after Israel's first king.

"All this," Paul said, "came to me by inheritance." He did nothing to gain it. He simply received this position by the fact that he was born into a religious race and family.

2. *His religious achievements*

Paul was no ordinary Hebrew, but a "Hebrew of Hebrews." He had worked hard to become a distinguished scholar, a man of letters and education. He spoke both Hebrew and Aramaic, a mark of distinction in Israel. Like a former Benjamite named Saul, who physically stood head and shoulders above his peers, Saul of Tarsus (though no doubt short of stature) stood "head and shoulders" above his fellow men in *religious* stature. Furthermore, Paul was a Pharisee, representing the most conservative sect within Judaism. Under Gamaliel, a renowned teacher, Paul had learned almost every jot and tittle of the law of Moses, along with all the traditions that had been added over the years.

Proof of Paul's commitment to the Pharisaic life and practice was his attitude toward Christians. He became an active persecutor of those who believed in Christ. On another occasion he wrote, "For you have heard of my previous way of life in Judaism, how I violently persecuted the church of God and tried to destroy it" (Gal. 1:13).

Finally, Paul capped his impressive list of achievements with what every serious Jew strove for — "legalistic righteousness." I was "faultless," he wrote. What was expected, he did. By man's evaluation, he had achieved the goal.

Thus Paul could boast — like no other Jew — about both his religious inheritance and his achievements. If man could be saved by works, he had it made. He did it all!

But Paul had a rude awakening. On the way to Damascus to imprison Christians, he met Jesus Christ, the One he was actually persecuting (Acts 9:1-6). Suddenly, miraculously, and to his shame, he discovered that everything he had done had not brought him one step closer to God or heaven. But this discovery changed the direction of his life — both on earth and eternally.

C. Paul's Present Experience (3:7-11).

Upon his conversion, Paul's religious experience and message shifted from being man-centered to being Christ-centered. In fact, in this final paragraph he mentioned Jesus Christ five times to describe his relationship with God; in the previous paragraph he had talked only about *his* inheritance and *his* achievements. As Paul concluded this section in his letter, he evaluated his past experience, then described his new source of righteousness, and finally stated his life goals as a Christian.

1. *His view of the past*

Paul evaluated his religious inheritance and accomplishments with strongly negative language. To him it was all a *total loss*. All his inheritance and all his achievements — "I consider them rubbish," he said (3:8).

Paul said this, not because most of these things were bad in themselves, but because they stood in the way of his personal relationship with God. Furthermore, his experience of knowing Christ was so much greater and more significant that he was willing to give up everything for this new experience — his citizenship, his status, his friends, and his wealth. He wrote it in no uncertain terms: "I consider *everything a loss*

compared to the surpassing greatness of knowing Christ
Jesus my Lord'' (3:8).

But there was another factor that caused Paul to use such
strongly negative language to describe his past experience.
His zeal against the Christians had been so ardent that he said
and did things that plagued his memory until the day he died.
He never forgot his terrible attitudes and behavior toward
Christians. Thus, when he wrote to the Corinthians, he said,
''For I am the least of the apostles and do not even deserve to
be called an apostle, because I persecuted the church of God''
(2 Cor. 15:9). Though his sins were totally forgiven, the
emotional scars were never erased.

2. *His new source of righteousness*

When Paul was converted, he discovered a new source of
righteousness — not the righteousness ''that comes from the
law, but that which is through faith in Christ — the righteousness that comes from God and is by faith'' (Phil. 3:9).
This, of course, was true righteousness because, Paul said
when writing to the Galatians, ''by observing the law *no one*
will be justified'' (Gal. 2:16).

Before he met Jesus Christ personally, Paul was a lost
man. His circumcision was meaningless; it was pure ritual.
Being a member of the chosen race did not make him a
member of the family of God. Being a Benjamite and an
outstanding Hebrew represented only a social, not a spiritual,
position. His extreme knowledge of the law only made him
more aware of sin and the inner conflict that raged in his soul
(Rom. 7:7-13).

Paul's ''legal righteousness'' was ''like a filthy garment''
in the sight of God (Isaiah 64:6 NASB). But now Paul could
claim with confidence a *true righteousness* — that which was
by faith apart from works. For the first time in his life, after
all his religious achievements, he realized that all men —
both in Old Testament days and New Testament days — were
justified by faith, not by the works of the law (Rom. 4:1-8).

3. *His new life goals*

Paul came to know Christ through his initial salvation experience, but "knowing Christ" is also to be an ongoing and growing experience. The apostle concluded this paragraph by saying: "I want *to know* Christ and the power of his resurrection and the fellowship of sharing in his sufferings, becoming like him in his death, and so, somehow, to attain to the resurrection from the dead" (3:10, 11).

These words of Paul have been interpreted in various ways. But one thing is sure: he was *not* talking about uncertainty regarding his salvation. If he were, he was contradicting everything he ever wrote about his eternal hope and expectation — even in the opening paragraphs of this very Epistle to the Philippians (1:19-23). Of course, his words to the Roman Christians represent his strongest statement of how he felt about his security in Christ: "For I am convinced that neither death nor life, neither angels nor demons, neither the present nor the future; nor any powers, neither height nor depth, nor anything else in all creation, will be able to separate us from the love of God that is in Christ Jesus our Lord" (Rom. 8:38, 39).

The most logical explanation seems to be that Paul was talking about his new life's goals; that is, to become like Christ in every aspect, even before he died, including Christ's resurrection life. This Paul acknowledged in the next paragraph was an impossible goal, for only through Christ's return will Christians be totally transformed into Christ's likeness (3:20, 21). But as will be seen in the next chapter, Paul did not allow this reality to deter him from the continuous process of coming to know Christ more deeply and profoundly in all aspects of his earthly life — His suffering, His death, and even His resurrection. Paul's ultimate goal was to reflect the *living and glorified Christ* in his present attitudes and actions.

A TWENTIETH-CENTURY APPLICATION

Paul's experience with a *man-centered religion* represents

millions of people today who are diligently striving to become worthy of going to heaven. Human effort — doing something to become worthy of heaven — is one characteristic that is true of all non-Christian religions and cults. From Hinduism, Buddhism, and Islam to Christian Science, Mormonism, Armstrongism, and Russellism (Jehovah's Witnesses) — *all* have one thing in common: a salvation based primarily on works.

There also are those involved in various forms of historic Christianity who are also relying upon works for salvation. Like Paul in his pre-conversion days, they are basing their salvation upon both religious inheritance and religious achievements. If you were to ask them if they are Christians, they might say, "Of course I'm a Christian! I was baptized as a baby." Or, "I was born in a Christian home; I've always been a Christian."

From the standpoint of achievement, they might say, "Of course I'm a good Christian. I go to church every Sunday." Or, "I read my Bible and pray every day." Or, "No one is perfect, but I keep the Ten Commandments the best I can." Or, "I give at least 10 percent of my money to the church."

For the most part, these practices are good and right. A Christian *should* read his Bible and pray. He *should* give his money to God's work as he has been prospered. He *should* go to church and learn the word of God and fellowship with other believers. He *should* be baptized, not to save his soul, but to demonstrate to others his conversion experience. But unfortunately many are relying upon these things to get them to heaven. There is only one way to heaven: by believing on Jesus Christ and by receiving Him as personal Savior (Acts 16:31; John 1:12). Have you had this experience? If not, this "Personal Life Response" is particularly for you.

A PERSONAL LIFE RESPONSE

Read the following statements and, if you can, fill in the blanks with your name:

"I, _____, acknowledge that I have received Jesus Christ as my personal Savior. I realize that I could never earn my salvation. My righteousness is not my own, but that which has been given to me through Christ's perfect sacrifice on the cross. Today, as an act of worship, I want to thank God for saving me from my sins — by grace through faith.

"But I, _____ as a Christian saved by grace, also want to acknowledge that with God's help I will do everything I can to live for Christ and to be like Christ — to obey His words and, like Paul, to come to know Him in all aspects of His life."

If you cannot write your name in the spaces sincerely and with meaning, pray the following prayer, and then you will be able to do so:

"I acknowledge that I am a sinner. I *have* fallen short of God's perfect standard for righteousness. I also acknowledge that Jesus Christ died for me, to give me perfect righteousness. I now receive Him as my personal Savior. I believe that He died for me and rose again to provide me with eternal life. Thank you, Jesus, for coming into my life."

Perhaps you found it easy to write your name in the first blank above, but you are having difficulty honestly writing your name in the second blank. If so, may I suggest that you read the following paraphrase of Romans 12:1, 2 as a covenant between you and God. If you will make this covenant, sign your name. Then you will have no difficulty filling in both blanks in the previous paragraphs.

"In view of God's mercy in sending Christ to die for me, I offer myself a living sacrifice, holy and pleasing to God — which is my spiritual worship. I no longer will allow my life to conform to the pattern of this

world, but will be transformed by the renewing of my mind so that I will be able to test and approve what God's will is — His good, pleasing, and perfect will.''
Signed _____.

INDIVIDUAL OR GROUP PROJECT

As parents, discuss this chapter and the Life Response with each member of your family who is old enough to understand the gospel. Note that a child of four or five years of age can clearly understand the basic elements of the gospel, when it is explained simply, and can invite Jesus Christ to be his or her Savior.

As an individual, prayerfully select a non-Christian friend and ask to share this chapter with him or her, and ask that person to consider making this Life Response.

NOTES

[1] Two things need to be said about Philippians 3:1. First, the human element in Paul's communication is frequently seen in other letters he wrote: compare Philippians 3:1 and 4:8, 9 with Ephesians 3:1 and 3:14. Note the sudden and spontaneous parentheses and digressions in his thought patterns.

This fact does not detract from their authoritiveness and place in the Holy Scriptures. It only bears witness to the miracle of inspiration — that is, as Christ was both God and man, so Scripture is both human and divine in its origin. If the Bible exhibited totally divine characteristics in its origin, it would be unrecognizable to human beings, for we have had no direct exposure to communication that is totally divine, that is, communication without human form and characteristics. On the other hand, for the Bible to be totally human would put it on a par with other literature, subject to error, inconsistency, and eventual extinction.

The second observation that must be made is that Paul no doubt had written to the Philippians about these matters on another occasion. If so, the letter is not available today, just as other letters which Paul wrote have been lost and are not included in Holy Scripture (see 2 Thess. 2:2, 15; 3:17; 2 Cor. 10:10,11). Conversely, perhaps the Philippians had access to another letter of Paul's — such as the one to the Galatians, which was written a number of years before Philippians. His statement in Philippians 3:1, however, reads: ''It is no trouble for me to write the same things *to you again.*'' This seems to militate against the possibility that he was referring to a letter written to another church.

² Paul also spoke very directly to fellow Christians who were allowing themselves to be led astray by these false teachers (see Gal. 3:1). This did not reflect "lack of love," but was evidence of *how much* he really loved them. The true test of love is whether or not people stop you when they know you are heading in the wrong direction. Sometimes it takes strong words — as every parent knows — for people to know what is being said and to recognize how serious the problem is.

³ Paul's word usage here in the original is highly significant. R. P. Martin points out that the apostle is referring "to the practice of circumcision; but Paul will not give it its proper name *'peritomē.'* Instead, by a pun, he mockingly calls it a mere cutting, *'katatomē,'* i.e., mutilation of the body on a par with pagan practices forbidden in Leviticus xxi. 5. . . . The same derision is applied to the Judaizers on Galatians v. 12, where *'apokoptein,'* 'to cut off' is a reference to their concern with the physical act of circumcision, and ironically means also 'to castrate.' The true name *'peritomē'* is reserved for Christians who are the circumcision." (R. P. Martin, *The Epistle of Paul to the Philippians*. Grand Rapids: Wm. B. Eerdmans Publishing Co., 1959, p. 137).

Chapter XII

Becoming Like Christ

SOMETHING TO THINK ABOUT

How does a Christian become more and more like Jesus Christ? How are *you* going about it — if you are?

Two major problems confront Christians in this aspect of their lives. First, some believe they can actually become like Christ in this life — that is, reach a state of perfection. Second, there are Christians who try all kinds of "push-button" approaches, attempting to achieve instant maturity.

Let us see what Paul believed about "becoming like Christ."

A LOOK AT PAUL'S LETTER . . .

Paul's Personal Illustration

3:12 Not that I have already obtained all this,

①   or have already been made perfect,
     but I press on to take hold of that for which
                  Christ Jesus took hold of me.

3:13 Brothers, I do not consider myself yet to have taken
     hold of it.
     But one thing I do:
       Forgetting what is behind and ②
       straining toward what is ahead, ③

3:14 I press on toward the goal to win the prize
          for which God has called me heavenward
            in Christ Jesus.

Paul's General Exhortation

3:15 All of us who are mature should take such a view of
     things. ①
     And if on some point you think differently, ②
       that too God will make clear to you.

3:16 Only let us live up to what we have already attained. ③

3:17 Join with others in following my example, brothers,
       and take note of those who live according to the
       pattern we gave you. ④

3:18 For, as I have often told you before
     and now say again even with tears, ⑤
     many live as enemies of the cross of Christ.

3:19 Their destiny is destruction,
       their god is their stomach, and
       their glory is in their shame.
       Their mind is on earthly things.

Paul's Ultimate Expectation

3:20 But our citizenship is in heaven.

3:20   And we eagerly await a Savior from there, ①
         the Lord Jesus Christ,
           who, by the power that enables him

3:21   to bring everything under his control, ②
     will transform our lowly bodies
       so that they will be like his glorious body.

WHAT DID PAUL SAY?

A. Paul's Personal Illustration
1. "I have not 'arrived' in my Christian experience."

2. "I do not look back to my previous experience."
3. "I keep looking and moving forward toward the goal of Christian maturity."

B. Paul's General Exhortation
1. "Don't be satisfied with *your* present level of Christian experience either."
2. "Be prepared to learn directly from the Lord."

3. "Don't inadvertently lose what you've gained because you *think* you have arrived."
4. "Follow good examples of Christian behavior."
5. "Be on guard against bad examples."

C. Paul's Ultimate Expectation
1. "Christ is coming."
2. "Christ will then totally transform us into His "likeness."

WHAT DID PAUL MEAN?

After his conversion, Paul turned from trying to become righteous by keeping the law to a new approach to life. Having discovered true righteousness through faith in Christ's death and resurrection, he set a new life goal — "to know Christ."

Stated alone, this goal would remain a vague generalization even if you knew that Paul was talking about knowing Christ experientially.[1] So the apostle spelled out what he meant: "I want to know Christ," he wrote, "and the power of his resurrection and the fellowship of sharing in his sufferings, becoming like him in his death, and so, somehow, to attain to the resurrection from the dead" (3:10, 11).

As pointed out in the previous chapter, Paul was not reflecting an uncertainty about his salvation. He *knew* he would go to be with Christ after death, and when Christ returned, he would receive a new body. Rather, Paul was stating a goal. He had a desire to reflect in *his* Christian life on earth all the qualities of Christ's life while *He* was on earth — even those characteristics that Christ reflected after He was raised from the dead.

But Paul was a realist! He knew this was an impossible goal for him or any Christian to reach in this life. Thus he cautioned the Philippian Christians to avoid getting caught in a legalistic trap, *even as believers*. He warned against the doctrine of "perfectionism" that has in fact sprung up here and there in the Christian community ever since New Testament days. This Paul did with a *personal illustration*, a *general exhortation*, and an accurate presentation of a Christian's *ultimate expectation*.

A. Paul's Personal Illustration (3:12-14)

There were some Christians in Philippi who no doubt thought Paul was teaching perfectionism — that is, that it is possible while on earth to "arrive" in the Christian life, to come to the place where you no longer sin. Since Paul often emphasized that Christians should live *like* Christ, and since Paul was such a tremendous example of *Christlike living,* it is understandable why some may have drawn this conclusion — especially if they took certain of his teachings out of context or listened to false teachers who deliberately perverted Paul's teachings.

Consequently Paul hastened to clarify his new life goal. To paraphrase these verses, Paul was saying: "I have not yet reached this goal. I have not yet become perfect like Christ. But it *is* my goal — even while on earth — to become like Christ, to become what he called me to be. As I said, I haven't reached it, but I have one burning desire — to be like Christ in every aspect of His life. I am not allowing my past life to drag me down. Rather, I am moving full speed ahead toward the goal. And in heaven, when Christ calls me home, I'll receive the prize — I'll be like Christ: that is, completely conformed to His image" (paraphrase of 3:12-14).

Observe Paul's personal illustration. It has often been stated or alluded to by various Christian leaders that to "become like Christ" involves various formulas. Some say, for example, that it involves the "faith-life." "Just relax!" some say. Or, "Let go and let God." Or, "Die to self and become alive to God."

More frequently we are told to "confess our sins and be filled with the Spirit." In each of these cases, the result is supposed to be a new and spontaneous level of spiritual victory — the secret to Christian living.

Don't misunderstand! All these statements have some validity. The Christian life *is* a life of faith; it *does* involve death to self and the old nature; it *does* mean a life lived in proper relationship to the Holy Spirit. In other words, it *does* involve a supernatural walk, drawing strength and power from Christ Himself. This is one reason why part of Paul's goal was to "know Christ and the *power* of his resurrection" — right then, in a Roman prison.

But note again Paul's personal illustration. "I press on toward the goal," he said. And this involves *"straining* toward what is ahead." These are strong, active words involving Paul himself. The analogy is a race — a runner looking straight ahead toward the finish line and putting every ounce of effort possible into the contest. Obviously Paul was exerting human energy to become like Christ; it involved *goal-setting, motivation,* and *personal action.* Here again is an illustration of that intricate balance between divine enablement and human responsibility. God never forces a man against his will to be conformed to the image of Christ; this is, I repeat, human responsibility.

The point is clear in Paul's Roman letter when Paul "urged" Christians — he did not demand or command them — "to offer yourselves as living sacrifices" (12:1).

The same is true in his letter to the Ephesians: "I *urge* you to live a life worthy of the calling you have received" (4:1). And then, reading on in this letter to the Ephesians, you discover that Paul told them *how* to live this kind of life. They were to *"make every effort* to keep the unity of the Spirit."* They were to "put off the old self" and to "put on the new self." More specifically, they were to "put off falsehood and speak truthfully." They were to "steal no longer," but rather "work, doing something useful." They were to "get rid of all bitterness, rage and anger, brawling and slander" and "be kind and compassionate" (Eph. 4:3, 22-32).

Obviously all this involves *human responsibility* and *personal action,* based on *new life goals.*

But Paul culminated the Ephesian letter once again with that unique balance between human responsibility and divine enablement. He said, *"Be strong* in the Lord and in His mighty power" (6:10). How does a Christian tap this power? He must "put on the full armor of God" (6:11).

Notice! Even the armor that Paul listed includes this balance. The "belt of truth," the "breastplate of righteousness," and the "gospel of peace" had already been defined in the Ephesian letter by Paul as human responsibility. To these Paul added the divine, supernatural elements: the "shield of faith," the "helmet of salvation," the "sword of the Spirit, which is the word of God." And they were "to pray in the Spirit on all occasions with all kinds of prayers and requests" (6:14-18).

To become Christlike involves a balance between human effort and relying upon divine resources. This Paul illustrated in his own life: "My goal is to know the reality of Christ's resurrection power in my life." But in essence he was saying, "I have not arrived in my Christian life; and I do not look back to my previous experience; rather I keep looking and pressing forward toward the goal of Christian maturity."

B. Paul's General Exhortation (3:15-19)

The apostle's personal illustration became the basis for a general exhortation to the Philippians. This exhortation can be summarized with a series of paraphrased statements. Let us look at these statements one by one.

   1. *"Don't be satisfied with* your *present level of Christian experience either."*

"All of us who are mature," Paul wrote, "should take such a view of things" (3:15a). That is, all Christians — even mature Christians — should never be satisfied with their present level of Christian experience and maturity. Above all, they should never feel they have reached the state of perfection.

Some Christians get confused about the fact that the Bible speaks of two levels of maturity. There is that ultimate maturity, that final heavenly state when all believers will receive new bodies created in Christ's image. This Paul referred to in Philippians 3:12, 21.

But there is also a level of recognizable maturity that can be achieved while on this earth — a maturity that reflects certain characteristics and qualities. Probably the most complete profile reflecting this maturity is found in 1 Timothy 3 and Titus 1. Here are qualities that Paul set forth for eldership. A close look at these qualities in context, however, reveals that these characteristics should be goals for every Christian. These qualities which reflect Christian maturity will be listed in the Life Response later in this chapter.

2. *"Be prepared to learn directly from the Lord."*

After reminding the Philippians that all mature Christians should have the same view on Christian maturity that Paul himself had toward his own life, he continued, "And if on some point you think differently, that too God will make clear to you" (3:15). Inherent in this statement is, it seems, God's supernatural strategy which He uses to reveal to Christians that they are not yet perfect. Paul stated it well to the Corinthians: "If you think you are standing firm, be careful that you don't fall!" (1 Cor. 10:12).

My personal experience has been (hasn't yours?) that God has a way of gently — and sometimes not so gently — pulling the rug out from under the Christian when self-righteous attitudes develop. I grew up in a legalistic church — a church where I was literally taught by direct statements and attitudes — that I was better than all other Christians because I was a member of that particular group. My self-righteous attitudes were so subtle that I didn't even recognize them — until God allowed me to get into a situation where I learned beyond a shadow of a doubt that I was no better than anyone else. In fact, I discovered through this experience that I was *weaker* than *most* Christians. In that time of great spiritual and psychological crisis I learned that I needed what other Christians had — the very Christians whom I thought were weaker than I.

3. *"Don't inadvertently lose what you've gained because you* think *you have arrived."*

In verse 16 Paul makes another statement that seems on the surface to be somewhat obscure: "Only let us live up to what we have already attained." Perhaps he was exhorting the Philippians not to backslide — not to go to the opposite extreme and practice license rather than legalism. But it seems more logical from the context to conclude that Paul was referring to what frequently goes along with legalistic perfectionism and a "holier-than-thou" attitude. Those who believe they have a corner on God's holiness are often the most divisive and argumentative. They are often unteachable and consequently violate the very truth they propound. By contrast, Paul said on another occasion that mature Christians "don't have anything to do with foolish and stupid arguments." They know that this kind of dialogue "produces quarrels." Instead, said Paul, a mature Christian "must be kind to everyone, able to teach, not resentful. Those who oppose him he must gently instruct, in the hope that God will give them a change of heart leading them to a knowledge of the truth" (2 Tim. 2:23-25).

4. *"Follow good examples of Christian behavior."*

Some Christians in Philippi must have been quite sure they had reached an ultimate level of maturity. They thought "they had arrived." This is undoubtedly why Paul shared his personal experience. The Philippians loved and respected this great man. For a spiritual giant like Paul to share with these people his own inadequacies and his own goals for spiritual development would have a significant impact on their view of their own spiritual status. Thus Paul exhorted, "Join with others in following my example, brothers" (3:17). That is, don't think you have arrived. Forget the things that are behind you and press on toward the goal to win the prize — your ultimate sanctification.

Paul further exhorted them to follow the example of others who followed this pattern in their lives, such as Timothy and Epaphroditus. Paul had already presented these two men as outstanding examples of Christian maturity (2:19-30), but as we've seen, both had human weaknesses. Both had physical and psychological problems that interfered with their effectiveness — even as mature Christian leaders.

5. *"Be on guard against bad examples."*

Paul once again warned against false teachers and worldly

minded people. With tears running down his cheeks, he called these worldlings "enemies of the cross of Christ" (3:18). This is a beautiful picture of Paul's attitudes and actions, even toward non-Christians who undermined and opposed his work. His language was strong, but his heart was broken. While weeping, he specified that "their destiny is destruction."

Three things, Paul said, characterized these enemies' life style. First, "their god is their stomach" — they were gluttons and drunkards; second, "their glory is in their shame" — they gloried in immorality and sensual behavior; and third, "their mind is on earthly things" — they were materialistic in their philosophy of life.

This, implied Paul, is the "pattern of this world." A mature and growing Christian does not allow his life to "conform" to this pattern, but rather be "transformed" and "renewed." Then, Paul said, "you will be able to test and approve what God's will is" (Rom. 12:2).[2]

C. Paul's Ultimate Expectation (3:20,21)

"No," Paul said, "we can never be perfect while living on this earth. But we can become more and more like Christ if we have His life style as our goal, striving toward this goal, following good examples rather than bad ones, and always maintaining a teachable attitude."

But there is more to the story. Someday every believer will be with Christ and have bodies that "will be like His glorious body." This was Paul's final word to the Philippians about perfection and sanctification.

Paul reminded the Philippians once again that their citizenship was really *in heaven – not in Philippi* as members of a Roman colony (1:27). Their savior was not the Roman emperor, who, since Julius Caesar, was proclaimed by some followers to be "the savior of mankind"; rather, the Lord Jesus Christ was their Savior. True, Christ had already saved them from their sins; but someday He would come to remove them totally from the world. The very power that enabled

Christ to "bring everything under his control" would transform them into His image. This, Paul said, will be our final and most significant prize at the end of the race. In this sense, there will be no losers.

A TWENTIETH-CENTURY APPLICATION

Today, as in the first century, many people are confused about spiritual maturity — *what* it is and *how* to get there. Some Christians still believe they can reach a state of perfection while on earth; most, however know they haven't "arrived," especially those who know them well, such as family members. And so do the Christians themselves, if they're honest. For those with this attitude, Paul gave a straightforward exhortation in this passage regarding what *is* a proper perspective on Christian maturity.

But the majority of Christians today have another problem. Many are trying all kinds of push-button formulas for achieving instant maturity: dying to self, living by faith, being filled with the Spirit. Along with these go the Bible reading and prayer formulas.

As stated earlier, there is truth in nearly all of these statements. But basic to all this is the process Paul spelled out so clearly in this passage. Becoming a spiritually mature Christian involves *goal-setting*, *motivation*, and *action*. Christians who are immature in certain aspects of their lives must deal with particular problems by first of all isolating the problem in the light of Scripture. Then they must translate that problem into a goal, striving to change that part of their lives while at the same time seeking God's help through faith, prayer, and meditation on the Word of God (Eph. 6:10-18).

There is no magical, push-button approach to becoming a mature Christian. Becoming like Christ is a process — a lifelong process.

A PERSONAL LIFE RESPONSE

The following project is designed to help you evaluate your maturity level as a Christian. The following questions and evaluation scale will help you to rate yourself in relation to qualities listed by Paul in 1 Timothy 3 and Titus 1. Circle the number that best represents your self-evaluation, rating from dissatisfied (1) to satisfied (7):[3]

	Dissatisfied						Satisfied

1. How do you evaluate your reputation as a Christian? Do people speak well of you?   1 2 3 4 5 6 7

2. How do you evaluate your overall relationship with your wife or husband? If you are not married, how well are you handling your social relationships — particularly, your sexuality?   1 2 3 4 5 6 7

3. What kind of overall perspective do you have on the Christian life? Have you developed a well-balanced biblical philosophy of life?   1 2 3 4 5 6 7

4. Are you prudent? That is, do you have a correct view of yourself in relationship to other Christians? in relationship to God?   1 2 3 4 5 6 7

5. Are you respectable? Do you have a well-adjusted life, adorning the Word of God?   1 2 3 4 5 6 7

6. Are you hospitable? Do you use your home as a means to minister to other members of the body in Christ as well as to non-Christians?   1 2 3 4 5 6 7

7. Are you able to teach? That is, do you have that quality of life that enables you to communicate the Word of God to others in a nonargumentative manner?   1 2 3 4 5 6 7

8. Are you addicted to anything that is controlling your life? Furthermore, are you doing anything that is caus-

ing a weaker Christian to stumble
and sin against God?   1 2 3 4 5 6 7

9. Are you self-willed? That is, do you
   always have to have your own way?   1 2 3 4 5 6 7

10. Do you lose your temper easily? Do
    you harbor feelings of resentment
    over a period of time?   1 2 3 4 5 6 7

11. Are you a pugnacious person — one
    who physically strikes out at others
    because of angry feelings?   1 2 3 4 5 6 7

12. Are you contentious? That is, do you
    purposely take the opposite point of
    view from others, stirring up argu-
    ments and destroying the unity in the
    group? Or are you a "peacemaker"
    striving to create harmony and unity?   1 2 3 4 5 6 7

13. Are you a mild-mannered and gentle
    person, reflecting meekness, forbear-
    ance, and kindness?   1 2 3 4 5 6 7

14. Are you free from the love of money?
    That is, do you seek first His kingdom
    and His righteousness?   1 2 3 4 5 6 7

15. Do you have your household in order?
    That is, do your wife and children
    love and respect you, and are they
    responding to your God and Savior
    and His claim on their lives?   1 2 3 4 5 6 7

16. Do you have a good reputation with
    non-Christians? That is, do they
    respect you even though they may
    disagree with your religious views?   1 2 3 4 5 6 7

17. Do you pursue what is good and
right? Do you desire to associate your-
self with truth, honor, and integrity?   1 2 3 4 5 6 7

18. Are you just? That is, are you able
to make objective decisions and be
honest in your relationships with
other people?   1 2 3 4 5 6 7

19. Are you pursuing personal and
practical holiness?   1 2 3 4 5 6 7

20. Are you in the process of continual
growth in your Christian life, becom-
ing more and more like Jesus Christ?   1 2 3 4 5 6 7

INDIVIDUAL OR GROUP PROJECT

Now that you have completed this project, I suggest that
you take two steps:

1. Discuss your self-evaluation with your wife or husband.
Identify your strengths as well as your weaknesses. If you
are single, share with a friend you love and trust.

2. The paperback entitled *The Measure of a Man* (Ventura,
Calif.: Regal Books, 1974) is designed to help you develop these qualities in your life. A chapter is devoted to
each quality with a personal project to help you develop
this quality in your life. As husband and wife, read a
chapter together each week and then work out the personal
projects at the end of each chapter.

If you circled "7" on each of the twenty questions, please
consult the Lord! You have a problem.

NOTES

[1] Paul had a choice of several Greek words to express the concept of
"knowledge." However, the word he chose to use (*gnōsis*) means
"spiritual knowledge." It implies more than just "head knowledge"; it is
knowledge that affects the total life.

[2] Some expositors believe Paul was speaking of Judaizers with these
descriptive statements. Perhaps this is true. If he was, he didn't seem to

consider them true believers. To be "enemies of the cross of Christ" whose "destiny is destruction" is a rather strong epithet to describe even a carnal Christian.

[3] For a more thorough study of these qualities and how to achieve them in your life, see *The Measure of a Man,* by Gene A. Getz (Ventura , Calif.: Regal Books, 1974).

Chapter XIII

Standing Firm

SOMETHING TO THINK ABOUT

Check yourself. How do you measure up?

	Never					Always	
1. Am I a Christian who is constantly working to create unity and understanding in the body of Christ?	1	2	3	4	5	6	7
2. Do I reflect a positive attitude toward trials and difficulties in my life?	1	2	3	4	5	6	7
3. Do I reflect an attitude of gentleness and graciousness toward non-Christians, even those who may persecute me?	1	2	3	4	5	6	7
4. Do I have real confidence in God and the power of prayer?	1	2	3	4	5	6	7
5. Do I regularly think about things that can be classified as excellent and praiseworthy?	1	2	3	4	5	6	7

A LOOK AT PAUL'S LETTER . . .

Stand Firm in the Lord
4:1 Therefore, my brothers,
① you whom I love and long for,
my joy and crown,
② that is how you should stand firm in the Lord,
dear friends!

Stand Firm in Unity and With Understanding
4:2 I plead with Euodia and I plead with Syntyche ①
to agree with each other in the Lord.
4:3 Yes, and I ask you, loyal yokefellow, help these ②
women
who have contended at my side in the
cause of the gospel,
along with Clement and
③ the rest of my fellow workers,
whose names are in the book of life

Stand Firm With a Proper Attitude in This World!
4:4 Rejoice in the Lord always.
I will say it again: Rejoice! ①
4:5 Let your gentleness be evident to all. — ②
The Lord is near.
4:6 Do not be anxious about anything, but in everything,
by prayer and petition, with thanksgiving,
present your requests to God.
③
4:7 And the peace of God,
which transcends all understanding,
will guard your hearts and your minds in Christ Jesus.
4:8 Finally, brothers, whatever is true, whatever is noble,
whatever is right, whatever is pure,
whatever is lovely, whatever is admirable, if anything is excellent or
④ praiseworthy —
think about such things.
4:9 Whatever you have learned or received
or heard from me, or seen in me —
put it into practice.
And the God of peace will be with you.

WHAT DID PAUL SAY?

A. Stand Firm in the Lord
  1. A backward look

  2. A forward look

B. Stand Firm in Unity and With Understanding
  1. Euodia and Syntyche

  2. An "anonymous" counselor

  3. Other members of the body of Christ in Philippi

C. Stand Firm With a Proper Attitude Toward Life in This World
  1. An attitude reflecting joy
  2. An attitude reflecting gentleness and graciousness

  3. An attitude reflecting confidence in God

  4. An attitude reflecting positive and right thinking

WHAT DID PAUL MEAN?

In the paragraphs preceding these, Paul discussed the secret to victorious Christian living as an *individual* member of the body of Christ. In the paragraphs before us now, he discusses the secret to victorious Christian living as a *local body* of believers.

Both experiences are necessary to be able to live effectively for Jesus Christ. Christian living is both individual and corporate (both personal and relational). No Christian will become mature in Christ by "running the race" all by himself. He will never be able to become conformed to Christ's image by isolating himself from other members of Christ's body. We *do* need each other.

In this passage, then, Paul gave the Philippians specific instructions to enable them as a local body of believers to *stand firm* in their Christian life and witness — to live victoriously for Jesus Christ amid this world system and environment.

A. Stand Firm in the Lord (4:1)

Paul's statement at the beginning of chapter 4 seems to be both a *summary* of what he has said in this epistle, as well as an *introduction* to what he was still going to say.

"Therefore, my brothers," he wrote, "you whom I love and long for, my joy and crown, that is how you should stand firm in the Lord, dear friends!"

Summarily speaking, Paul went all the way back to the beginning of this letter when he spoke of his *joy* and *love* and *longing* for the Philippians. Earlier he had said: "In all my prayers for all of you, I always pray with *joy*" (1:4). He added, "God can testify how I *long* for all of you with the *affection* of Christ Jesus" (1:8).

Thus, Paul began the culmination of this letter by parenthetically reminding the Philippian Christians of his deep relationship and friendship with them. But his *primary concern* was that they "stand firm in the Lord!" Again, in summarizing, Paul emphasized in 4:1 that he had been laying out a strategy in the previous paragraphs for mature and victorious Christian living. He said, "Therefore, my brothers, . . . that is *how* you should stand firm in the Lord."

1. *A backward look*

This strategy on *how* to "stand firm" can be clearly summarized by the following six basic exhortations that Paul gave as he penned this epistle:

— "Whatever happens, conduct yourselves in a manner worthy of the gospel of Christ" (1:27a).

— "Stand firm in one spirit, contending as one man for the faith of the gospel without being frightened in any way by those who oppose you" (1:27b, 28a).

— "Do nothing out of selfish ambition or vain conceit, but in humility consider others better than yourselves. Each of you should look not only to your own interests, but also to the interests of others. Your attitude should be the same as that of Christ Jesus" (2:3-5).

— "Continue to work out your salvation with fear and trembling; . . . do everything without complaining or arguing" (2:12b, 14).

— "Watch out for those dogs, those men who do evil, those mutilators of the flesh" (3:2).

— "Join with others in following my example, brothers, and take note of those who live according to the pattern we gave you" (3:17).

The key phrase in 4:1 is that a Christian — in order to win the battle against Satan and the world — must "stand firm *in the Lord*." Again, this thrust reminds us of Paul's final words to the Ephesian Christians. He wrote, "Finally, be strong *in the Lord* and in *his* mighty power" (Eph. 6:10). No Christian will ever win the race purely in his own strength and through human effort.

2. *A forward look*

Philippians 4:1, then, is a summary statement — a concise reminder of the strategy Paul had already clearly presented and illustrated. But this verse is also introductory — a transitional statement to prepare the Philippians for some final thoughts and exhortations.

B. Stand Firm in Unity and With Understanding (4:2,3)

Maintaining oneness as Christians and striving for mutual understanding are dominant emphases in this letter, as seen in the preceding exhortations. Paul commended the Philippians for the degree of love and unity they had already achieved (1:9-11).

To this point, Paul spoke generally to the Christians at Philippi. He did not become personal. But as he concluded this epistle, he spoke directly to several people, calling them by name — people who were in a position to be instruments for helping to create even greater love and unity in the Philippian church.

1. *Euodia and Syntyche*

The first two people Paul mentioned were Euodia and Syntyche, two women who were having some kind of difficulty understanding each other. They were both committed and dedicated Christians, because, Paul said, they "have contended at my side in the cause of the gospel" (4:3).

This kind of disagreement, of course, is not unusual in a local body of believers. Paul understood it very well, for he, too, had had several confrontations with fellow Christians. On one occasion he had an open and frank disagreement with the apostle Peter over a theological issue (Gal. 2:11-14). On another occasion he dialogued with Barnabas over a practical issue — Should they or should they not take John Mark on the second missionary journey? — because John Mark had "deserted them" on the previous trip. Paul said no. But Barnabas said yes. Result? Barnabas took John Mark and went in one direction, and Paul chose Silas and went another way.

Not seeing eye to eye, then — even among mature Christians — is not a new phenomenon. But *mature* Christians also resolve their disagreements and come to mutual understanding and consensus. They do not allow these problems to interfere with love and unity in the body of Christ.

This, it seems, is what Paul was pleading for when he asked Euodia and Syntyche "to agree with each other in the Lord." Both were outstanding Christian women, but they needed to resolve their differences through open communication and mutual understanding.

2. An "anonymous" counselor

Notice that Paul recognized the women's need for help from another member of the body. No matter how mature we become as Christians, we all tend toward subjective reasoning and actions. We may need a third person or persons who can listen to both sides of the issue and bring about objectivity. Thus Paul exhorted a third member of the church — a person he could trust — to help these women resolve the tension that existed between them (4:2).[1]

3. Other members of the body of Christ in Philippi

The last person Paul mentioned by name was Clement — a man who along with Euodia and Syntyche had served faithfully with Paul. Paul referred anonymously to several other "fellow workers" and paid them the highest tribute any Christian could give to another. Their names, he said, were "in the book of life." The implication, of course, is that the really important place to find your name is not in a letter written by an apostle, but in the book of life, where every true Christian's name is recorded.

C. Stand Firm With a Proper Attitude Toward Life in This World (4:4-9)

Paul had already spoken to this issue specifically. But as he concluded this letter, he wanted to reinforce what he had already said with some additional words of encouragement and exhortation. Remember, he implied, if you want to be victorious as a body of believers, you must maintain certain attitudes and actions.

1. *Maintain an attitude reflecting joy*

"Rejoice in the Lord always. I will say it again: Rejoice!" (4:4). If any *one* word can be considered a key word in this letter, it is the word *joy* or *rejoice*. Paul used this expression several times to indicate his own attitude toward *all* circumstances. He prayed with *joy* (1:4). He *rejoiced* in his imprisonment because this experience was actually helping to spread the gospel (1:18). Furthermore, he *rejoiced* because he had confidence in the prayers of the Philippians and the Lord's power to make it possible for him to stand true to his Christian convictions, no matter what happened to him personally (1:18, 19).

Paul also referred to the *joy* the Philippians should experience as a result of his possible return to Philippi (1:26). On the other hand, they were to *rejoice* in the fact that he may *never* return, but rather have the privilege of dying for Christ (2:17, 18). When Epaphroditus returned to Philippi, they were to "welcome him in the Lord with great *joy!*" (2:29).

Finally, Paul came back to a cardinal point in his own Christian philosophy of life: *"Rejoice* in the Lord *always"* (3:1; 4:4). This was the major lesson Paul had learned personally, and the lesson he wanted to share with his Christian friends at Philippi. He said it well when he wrote, "I have learned the secret of being content in any and every situation" (4:12).

James wrote about the same attitude to Christians who were suffering persecution. "Consider it pure *joy,* my brothers, whenever you face trials of many kinds, because you know that the testing of your faith develops perseverance. Perseverance must finish its work so that you may be mature and complete, not lacking anything" (James 1:2-5).

2. *Maintain an attitude of gentleness and graciousness*

The context in Philippians 4 implies that Christians should not only be gentle and gracious among Christians, but also in their relationships with non-Christians. Thus Paul wrote, "Let your gentleness be evident to *all"* (4:5). Again, Paul had spoken to this issue before (2:14-16). But he wanted to reinforce this exhortation, and he obviously wanted to add this additional thought: "The Lord is near" (4:5b). It seems clear that Paul was referring to what he had spelled out in detail when he wrote to the Roman Christians, "Do not repay anyone evil for evil. Be careful to do what is right in the sight of *everybody*. If it is possible, as far as it depends on you, live at peace with *everyone*. Do not take revenge, my friends, but leave room for God's wrath, for it is written: 'It is mine to avenge, I will repay,' says the Lord. On the contrary: 'If your *enemy* is hungry feed him; if he is thirsty, give him something to drink. In doing this, you will heap burning coals on his head.' Do not be overcome by evil, but overcome evil with good" (Rom. 12:17-21).

In essence, Paul was saying to the Philippians, "Don't try to judge unbelievers. Leave that to the Lord. He is coming soon, and when He does, He will make everything right. In the meantime, be a gentle, gracious Christian."

3. *Maintain an attitude of confidence in God*

What then can a Christian do when he is surrounded with problems, persecution, and pain? Paul focused on a specific solution he had not yet shared with the Philippians — the power and healing of corporate prayer. "Do not be anxious about *anything*," he wrote, "but in *everything*, by prayer and petition, with thanksgiving, present your requests to God" (4:6).

Note that I said *corporate* prayer! All the way through this passage, and most of this epistle, Paul seemed to be referring to the body of Christ, not individual Christians per se. In many references to prayer in his other epistles, he mentioned praying in the context of "corporate prayer" — praying for one another — e.g., Romans 12:10-13; 1 Thessalonians 5:14-18.

Here in Philippians Paul was talking about bearing one another's burdens in prayer. Don't hesitate to voice your needs, he implied. Don't be afraid and anxious. Pray for each other.

Too long we have told Christians to pray about their problems in isolation. This often leads to more anxiety and discouragement. But mutual "burden-bearing" and concern help to ease the load and often bring about unusual psychological and even physical healing. This, implied Paul, is one way to tap the "peace of God, which transcends all understanding" (4:7).

Many events in life — some may represent minor things — create anxiety that can never be relieved through a purely rational and logical approach to problem-solving. True Christianity is reflected when a believer is able to trust God and other members of the body of Christ, even when it is beyond his human ability to understand. Thus a man of great wisdom once wrote, "Trust in the Lord with all your heart, and do not lean on your own understanding. In all your ways acknowledge Him, and He will make your paths straight" (Prov. 3:5, 6 NASB).

4. *Maintain an attitude of positive and right thinking*

Norman Vincent Peale was not the first man to capitalize on the psychological law of "positive thinking." Paul laid claim to this truth in the first century. In this letter he used a variety of words to describe those things which are excellent or praiseworthy and which Christians ought to think about.

The list is not comprehensive, but rather suggestive and illustrative. Also, the words are somewhat difficult to define in isolation. But together they form a positive profile for thought and action.

Notice, too, that Paul did not spell out specific "content" to think about. Rather, he listed qualities that could be used as criteria in every culture and at any given moment in history, thus making these virtues supracultural and timeless. Paul asked:

    a. Is it *true?* That is, is it true in the broadest sense of the term?

    b. Is it *noble?* That is, is it worthy of reverence?

    c. Is it *right?* Moral, upright, righteous?

    d. Is it *pure?* Chaste, characterized by purity?

e. Is it *lovely?* Winsome, pleasing, amiable?

f. Is it *admirable?* Winning, attractive?

After listing these qualities, Paul seemed to imply, ''You can add to this list if you like, but make sure your additions represent excellence or praiseworthiness. This is the *ultimate* criterion! Whatever you add, carefully meditate and think about the things that reflect these virtues.''

Paul concluded this paragraph by referring again to his own example, ''Whatever you have learned or received or heard from me, or seen in me — put it into practice.'' Paul laid his own reputation on the line. Essentially he said to the Philippians what he said to the Corinthians: ''Follow my example, as I follow the example of Christ'' (1 Cor. 11:1).

This was no pious sermon, but an exhortation that could be verified by any person who really knew Paul. Those who knew him well received the message as it was meant — a statement of humility, reflecting a heart that longed after God and ultimate sanctification.

Finally, Paul tied the exhortation to think on excellent and praiseworthy things to his previous exhortation to pray about everything. ''When you do these things,'' he implied, ''that is, if you trust God and pray about everything, and if you think positively on excellent and praiseworthy things, you will experience God's presence and peace'' (4:9).

A TWENTIETH-CENTURY APPLICATION

The best way, it seems, to apply Paul's first-century instructions to our lives today is to consider these exhortations as a criterion by which we can evaluate our level of Christian maturity — how well we are standing firm in the Lord.''

1. Am I a Christian who is constantly working toward creating unity and understanding in the body of Christ?

2. Do I reflect an attitude of joy in all circumstances? (The opposite of joy is complaining, arguing, fretting, moping, feeling sorry for one's self.) Biblical joy means having a positive attitude toward the problem, accepting it as a

challenge, attempting to see what God is trying to teach and what real value can come out of this experience personally.

3. Do I reflect an attitude of gentleness and graciousness toward non-Christians, even those who may persecute me?

4. Do I have real confidence in God and the power of prayer? Am I sharing with various members of the body of Christ those needs and concerns that I have for prayer? And am I a faithful Christian who prays for other members of the body of Christ?

Note that some 20th-century Christians misinterpret Paul's instructions. Some people share with other Christians what they consider a personal need — for example, a need for material help. Perhaps they should be asking Christians to pray that God would help them overcome the sin of laziness. The Bible is clear on this problem: to the Thessalonian Christians Paul wrote, "If a man will not work, he shall not eat" (2 Thess. 3:10).

Obviously there are real material needs even in the twentieth century. But it is also up to the leaders of the church to scrutinize what may be classified as material needs. They are responsible not to allow any Christian (or non-Christian) to take advantage of the graciousness of the other members of the body of Christ.

There are also some Christian workers today being supported by other Christians but taking advantage of the situation. In some instances, there is a lack of adequate supervision and accountability. This is why it is a good policy for a Christian to give his money through a recognized channel, such as a local church or reputable Christian organization. Then he will know the money is well spent and that individuals who receive financial assistance are held accountable for their time and effort.

5. Do I think positively about things that can be classified as excellent and praiseworthy? That is, are the things that

occupy my thought-life *true, noble, right, pure, lovely,* and *admirable?*

A PERSONAL LIFE RESPONSE

Read these questions again. Which one would classify as citing your greatest need? Select that one and write out a specific, achievable goal. Begin today to work toward that goal. Perhaps the place to start is to ask someone whom you trust in the body of Christ to pray that you will be able — with God's help — to achieve this goal.

INDIVIDUAL OR GROUP PROJECT

Use this passage of Scripture, the Application, and the Life Response, as a basis for discussion with your family or close friends. Perhaps one of these questions applies specifically to problems in your family (or group) as a whole. For example, discuss your "television viewing" habits, your "radio listening" habits, or your attitudes as a group.

NOTES

[1] There is some confusion as to whether or not Paul was naming a person in this verse or merely referring to someone anonymously. Relative to this problem, R. P. Martin comments, "He is designated rather curiously as true yokefellow which may be either a descriptive tribute to a Christian whose identity is concealed from us; or the two words may be taken together as a proper name: 'Syzygos (comrade), truly so called.' . . . If we assume that the Greek 'gnēsie suzuge' is to be translated as a proper name, the pun will find a parallel in the case of Onesimus in the letter to Philemon (cf. Philemon verse 11 for the play on the name which means 'useful, profitable'). In the case of 'Syzygos' Paul is playfully reminding him to be true to his name, and be a real 'yokefellow,' in assisting in the coming together of the estranged women. If there is no pun, and the title hides the real name of another Christian, we have no means of knowing who it was." (R. P. Martin, *The Epistle of Paul to the Philippians*. Grand Rapids: Wm. B. Eerdmans Publishing Co., 1959, p. 166).

Chapter XIV
Paul's Final Words

SOMETHING TO THINK ABOUT

If Paul were to write a letter and mention your personal attitudes and actions regarding your material possessions, what would he say? What would he say about your attitude toward money? What would he say about the amount you give "regularly" to the Lord's work?

What Paul said about his own attitudes and those of the Philippian Christians is *really* "something to think about."

A LOOK AT PAUL'S LETTER . . .

Paul's Philosophy of Self-Preservation

4:10 I rejoice greatly in the Lord
   that at last you have renewed your concern for me.
Indeed, you have been concerned,
   but you had no opportunity to show it.   ①

4:11 I am not saying this because <u>I am in need</u>, for I have ②
   learned to be <u>content whatever the circumstances.</u>

4:12 I know what it is to be in need, and I know what it is to ③
   have plenty. I have learned the secret of being content
   in any and every situation, whether well-fed or hungry, whether living in plenty or in want.

4:13 I can do everything through him who gives me
   strength.   ④

Paul's Final Commendation

4:14 Yet it was good of you to share in my troubles.

4:15 Moreover, as you Philippians know, in the early days
   of your acquaintance with the gospel, when I set out
   from Macedonia, <u>not one church shared with me in</u>   ①
   the matter of giving and receiving, <u>except you only;</u>

4:16 for even when I was in Thessalonica,
   you sent me aid again and again when I was in need.

4:17 Not that I am looking for a gift, but I am looking for
   what may be credited to your account.

4:18 I have received <u>full payment</u> and <u>even more;</u>   ②
   I am <u>amply supplied</u>, now that I have received from
   Epaphroditus the gifts you sent. They are a fragrant
   offering, an acceptable <u>sacrifice pleasing to God.</u>

4:19 And my God will meet all your needs   ③
   according to his glorious riches in Christ Jesus.

4:20 To our God and Father be glory for ever and ever.
   Amen.

Paul's Final Salutation

4:21 <u>Greet all</u> the saints in Christ Jesus.
   The brothers who are with me send greetings.

4:22 <u>All the saints send you greetings,</u>
   especially those who belong to Caesar's household.

4:23 The grace of the Lord Jesus Christ be with your spirit.

WHAT DID PAUL SAY?

A. Paul's Philosophy of Self-Preservation
1. Humility

2. Honesty

3. Adaptability

4. Certainty

B. Paul's Final Commendation
1. Exceptional commitment

2. Abundant giving

3. Sacrificial spirit

C. Paul's Final Salutation

WHAT DID PAUL MEAN?

Paul actually ended this letter where he began. Though it is somewhat hidden and obscure, in his introductory paragraphs he alluded to the material gifts the Philippians had sent him on a regular basis since the church was first launched in Philippi. "I always pray with joy," he said, "because of your partnership in the gospel from the *first* day until *now*" (1:4, 5). Probably Paul was referring here to the Philippians' constant support, not only in prayer, but also in material things.

So as Paul culminated his letter — an epistle prompted in the first place primarily by the gifts he had received from the Philippians via the hands of Epaphroditus — he thanked them specifically for their kindness and generosity. But in the process of saying a sincere "thank you," he shared another beautiful lesson from his own life: his personal philosophy regarding *self-preservation*, particularly as it related to material possessions.

A. Paul's Philosophy of Self-Preservation (4:10-13)

Paul's attitude and behavior regarding his material needs can be simply stated: he was *humble, honest,* and *adaptable* — with a *strong faith* in Christ to meet all his needs.

1. *Paul's humility*

"I rejoice greatly in the Lord," Paul wrote, "that at last you have renewed your concern for me. Indeed, you have been concerned, but you had no opportunity to show it" (4:10).

Paul seldom talked about *his* needs, but when he had one he admitted it. There was no subtle pride in his personality that was injured because of his lack of "things." He didn't go around trying to be something he wasn't. He lived within his means, and when he lacked he was not too proud to accept help.

As he wrote to the Philippians thanking them for their

gifts, he reflected this humility. He was *rejoicing* — there's his favorite word again — that they had once more helped him in a time of need. Indeed, he let them know that he had missed their help for a period of time, but quickly and sensitively communicated to them that he knew they had never stopped being concerned. Rather, he said, "you had no opportunity to show it."

It is possible only to speculate as to why the Philippians had temporarily stopped supporting Paul materially. Perhaps they did not know about his needs in Rome. Maybe they themselves were so poverty-stricken they could not possibly help. Whatever the reason, Paul wanted them to know he understood, but was excited about their renewed help.

2. *Paul's honesty*

Along with his humility went honesty — an important balance in forming a philosophy about material needs. After letting the Philippians know how happy he was about the gift they had sent, he hurried to tell them he was not playing on their sympathy. "I am not saying this because I am in need," he wrote (4:11).

How different from some Christians who methodically work at giving the impression they are *always* in need. Christian workers who make their living doing religious work can be especially tempted to take advantage of other members of Christ's body.

Paul was vitally concerned that his motives *never* be misinterpreted. On some occasions he actually refused what was coming to him as an apostle of Christ to avoid being a stumbling block to some Christians or to new babes in Christ (1 Cor. 9:1-18; 1 Thess. 2:9).

When it comes to having a Christian philosophy regarding material possessions, there is no substitute for honesty and integrity. On the one hand, a Christian need not be ashamed because his material possessions are not as great as someone else's. On the other hand, a Christian who is helped by other members of the body of Christ must never take advantage of the situation. Paul had no use for a lazy Christian.

Pointedly Paul dealt with this issue in Thessalonica: "For even when we were with you, we gave you this rule: 'If a man will not work, he shall not eat.' We hear that some among you are idle. They are not busy; they are busybodies. In the name of the Lord Jesus Christ, we command and urge such people to settle down and earn the bread they eat" (2 Thess. 3:10-12).

3. *Paul's Adaptability*

Paul had an unusual capacity to adapt to various situations and circumstances and still reflect contentment. "I know what it is to be in need," he wrote. "And I know what it is to have plenty." But he added, "I have learned the secret of being content in *any* and *every* situation (4:12).

The "situations" that Paul wrote about here involved his material needs — being "well-fed or hungry," "living in plenty or in want." It is one thing to be happy and content when we have food on the table, clothes on our backs, shelter over our heads, and some money in the bank. But what if all of these things were missing? How content would we be? How well could *we* adapt? Paul could say, "I have learned to be content *whatever* the circumstances."

Most tragic is the Christian who has abundance of everything and is yet unhappy and discontent. For this indiviaual, material blessings wear thin. His needs are far deeper. Far down inside are emotional and spiritual needs that all the money in the world won't and can't meet. Try as he may to find satisfaction, he will never succeed.

Fortunate indeed is the Christian who first of all seeks God's "kingdom and righteousness" (Matt. 6:33). All else will fail and grow thin. But when the deeper needs of man are met first, material possessions can come and go, yet the "house" will stand firm. It is built on a rock — not sand (Matt. 7:24-27).

4. *Paul's certainty*

Paul's ultimate secret was his profound trust and confidence in Jesus Christ. After explaining his philosophy, he wrote, "I can do everything through him who gives me strength" (4:13).

The "everything" does not mean that Paul believed he was some kind of superman — a miracle worker who could "leap tall buildings with a single bound." He meant he could face every situation involving material needs and still maintain a positive and victorious attitude toward the circumstances of life.

The apostle did not say that God always *met* his *material* needs. Not at all! Rather, Paul was certain that no matter what the circumstances — "whether well-fed or hungry, whether living in plenty or in want" — in every situation Christ would help him maintain an attitude of trust, confidence, and contentment. This was the *need* he was talking about.

B. Paul's Final Commendation (4:14-20)

Paul was a great believer in maintaining a ministry of encouragement. As he concluded this letter, he commended the Philippians for their *exceptional commitment* as compared with other churches, the *abundant gifts* which they had sent him, and their *sacrificial spirit* — their willingness to give even when their own material needs were not being met.

1. *Their exceptional commitment*

"It was good of you to share in my troubles," Paul wrote (4:14). "Moreover, . . . when I set out for Macedonia, not one church shared with me in the matter of giving and receiving, except you only; for even when I was in Thessalonica [Paul's next major place of ministry after he left Philippi], you sent me aid again and again when I was in need" (4:15, 16).

Paul did not hesitate to give honor when honor was due. This was part of his personal philosophy of ministry (Rom. 13:6, 7). He did not hesitate to let all Christians of all time know that the Philippian church was an outstanding body of believers who demonstrated an exceptional dedication when it came to giving.

2. *Their abundant giving*

The Philippians had "outdone themselves" in their ministry to Paul. They were not concerned about going over the top. They knew that if more were given than the need at the moment demanded, it would be used wisely and discreetly by their friend and brother in Christ. Consequently Paul wrote, "I have received full payment and even more; I am amply supplied, now that I have received from Epaphroditus the gifts you sent" (4:18).

3. *Their sacrificial spirit*

The gifts the Philippians had sent to Paul were "a fragrant offering, an acceptable sacrifice, pleasing to God" (4:18).

Do not misunderstand! Paul did not refer to quantity when he said, "I have received full payment and even more." Rather, he spoke of gifts that were given sacrificially by the church *as a whole*. Some in the Philippian church actually gave out of their "poverty" (2 Cor. 8:2); others gave out of their "plenty." But in God's sight, as a body they gave sacrificially. Whether the gift was a piece of fruit carefully nurtured by the converted slave girl and picked just at the right time to be ripe when it arrived in Rome, or whether it was a carefully woven cloak made by Lydia herself out of the finest fabrics in Philippi, in God's sight the gifts were "a fragrant offering, an acceptable sacrifice."

In God's sight, therefore, the amount in itself is not important. In today's culture, a dollar given sacrificially may be a more "fragrant offering" to our Lord than a $1,000 gift by someone who would never miss it. For some people, a dollar gift is a sacrifice; for someone else a $1,000 gift may merely be a tax deduction. Which do you think God will honor more?

Tax deductions are legitimate and important. Every Christian should take advantage of what is legally due him. The point I make here is one of "motivation." To give primarily to get a tax deduction is not the highest motivation and is more honoring to one's self than to God.

C. Paul's Final Salutation (4:21-23)

There is little need to comment on Paul's final greeting and farewell. It is clear, straightforward, and comprehensive. It reflects Paul's belief in true unity among all Christians who have put their faith in Christ Jesus. Paul was not parochial, denominational, and exclusive in his attitudes. *All believers* in Jesus Christ are *one* in Jesus Christ. All are related to each other. Consequently he said in closing:

"Greet all the saints in Christ Jesus. The brothers who are with me send greetings. All the saints send you greetings, especially those who belong to Caesar's household. The grace of the Lord Jesus Christ be with your spirit" (4:21-23).

A TWENTIETH-CENTURY APPLICATION

Paul's thrust in these final paragraphs in his Philippian letter seems to apply in two distinct but inseparable ways to Christians who live in the twentieth century. First there is an *individual* application; second, a *corporate* application. The following questions will help you make both:

1. As an individual, what is my personal philosophy regarding material possessions?
   a. Am I characterized by *humility, honesty, adaptability,* and *certainty* — thanking God for what I have and never using my possessions to lord it over others?
   b. If I do not have as much as others, am I constantly intimidated, or perhaps even somewhat jealous down deep? Or, do I thank God that I am first of all a member of the body of Christ, a co-heir with Jesus (Rom. 8:17), a child of the King? No matter what my material possessions, I can be an important member of the body of Christ alongside others who may have more material possessions than I have.

2. As a body of believers, are we demonstrating *exceptional commitment?* Are we demonstrating *abundant giving* and a *sacrificial spirit* with every member giving as God has prospered him?
   The words of Paul to the Corinthians are sufficient to help us evaluate our *individual* and *corporate* maturity in this

area. "Remember this: Whoever sows sparingly will also reap sparingly, and whoever sows generously will also reap generously. Each man should give what he has decided in his heart to give, not reluctantly or under compulsion, for God loves a cheerful giver. And God is able to make all grace abound to you, so that in all things at all times, having all that you need, you will abound in every good work" (2 Cor. 9:6-8).

A PERSONAL LIFE RESPONSE

As an individual, evaluate your personal philosophy regarding material things. If you are a leader in your church, help others evaluate their corporate philosophy regarding possessions and giving. Do you as an individual — does the church you are a part of — measure up to biblical standards for giving?

Read the Application questions again. Underscore any touching on matters in which you believe you personally or your church have been negligent. Then write out several significant steps you can take to correct the situation. For example, you may want to give more on a regular basis. Or, you may wish to cut back your spending on pure luxuries and give more to the Lord's work. You may wish to make a careful study of your total financial situation, evaluating your income and spending.

INDIVIDUAL OR GROUP PROJECT

Make a careful study of your financial situation, evaluating your income and spending. Do you know where your money is going? Do you have a budget in order to be a good steward of God's gifts to you? Do you have a definite system in making sure you are giving proportionately and regularly to the Lord's work?

The New Testament puts all Christians under grace. We are not obligated to give a certain percentage as believers were in the Old Testament. But the temptation is to take advantage of God's grace — particularly if we do not keep accurate records and give according to a set plan. If we give only as the Spirit moves, we may be moved only by our own spirit, which tends to be self-deceptive.

THE BIBLICAL RENEWAL SERIES
by
Gene A. Getz

ONE ANOTHER SERIES

Building Up One Another
Encouraging One Another
Loving One Another
Praying for One Another
Serving One Another

THE MEASURE OF SERIES

Measure of a . . .
  Church
  Family
  Man
  Woman

PERSONALITY SERIES

When You're Confused and Uncertain (Abraham)
When You Feel Rejected (Joseph)
When Your Goals Seem Out of Reach (Nehemiah)
When the Job Seems Too Big (Joshua)
When You Feel Like a Failure (David)
When the Pressure's On (Elijah)
When You Feel You Haven't Got It (Moses)

BIBLE BOOK SERIES

Pressing on When You'd Rather Turn Back
(Philippians)
Saying No When You'd Rather Say Yes
(Titus)
Believing God When You Are Tempted to Doubt
(James 1)
Doing Your Part When You'd Rather Let God Do It All
(James 2-5)
Looking Up When You Feel Down
(Ephesians 1-3)
Living for Others When You'd Rather Live for Yourself
(Ephesians 4-6)
Standing Firm When You'd Rather Retreat
(1 Thessalonians)

Partners for Life: Making a Marriage That Lasts